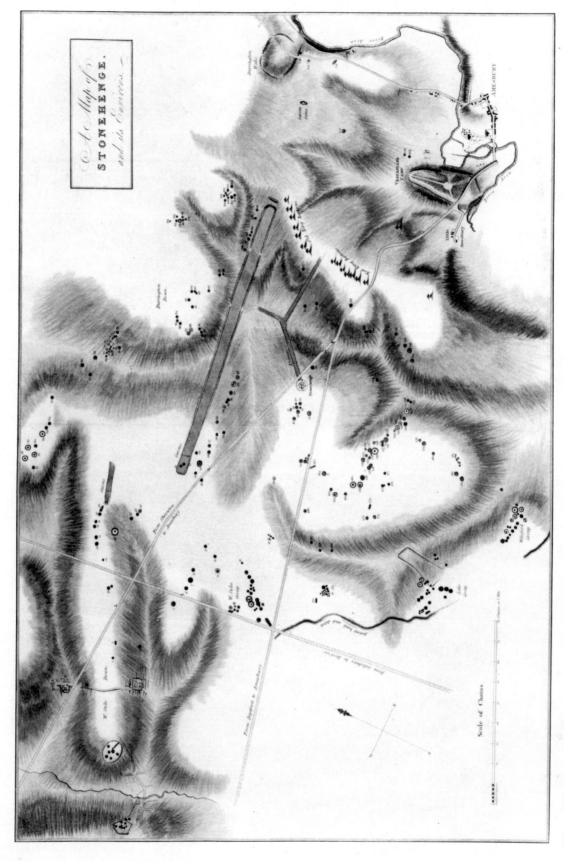

Plate 1. The first ARCHAEOLOGICAL MAP of the Stonehenge area, *from* Sir Richard Colt Hoare's *Ancient Wiltshire*, Part 1 (1810)

ROYAL COMMISSION ON HISTORICAL MONUMENTS
ENGLAND

STONEHENGE
AND ITS ENVIRONS

MONUMENTS AND LAND USE

5938-

EDINBURGH
AT THE UNIVERSITY PRESS
1979

© Crown copyright 1979
Published by Edinburgh University Press
for Royal Commission on Historical Monuments (England)

ISBN 0 85224 379 0

Set in Great Britain by Speedspools, Edinburgh
and printed by The Scolar Press Ltd, Ilkley, Yorks

Title page. BUSH BARROW in the early eighteenth century, with the sheep pen upon it; view NE to Stonehenge, *after* Stukeley (1740, Tab. XXXIII)

CONTENTS

'It commands a fine view.' said his companion, looking around him.
'True: but it is not for the prospect I brought you hither; do you see nothing else remarkable? nothing on the surface of the ground?'
'Why, yes; I do see something like a ditch, indistinctly marked.'
'Indistinctly! – pardon me, sir, but the indistinctness must be in your powers of vision. Nothing can be more plainly traced – a proper agger *or* vallum, *with its corresponding ditch or* fossa. . . . *Indistinct! – why, you must suppose that fools, boors, and idiots, have ploughed up the land, and, like beasts and ignorant savages, have thereby obliterated two sides of the square, and greatly injured the third; but you see, yourself, the fourth side is quite entire!'*

Sir Walter Scott, *The Antiquary* (1816)

This together with the several views I have drawn of it, will give us nearly as good a notion of the whole, as we can at this day expect, and perhaps preserve the memory of it hereafter, when the traces of this mighty work are obliterated with the plough, which it is to be fear'd will be its fate. That instrument gaining ground too much, upon the ancient and innocent pastoritial life; hereabouts, and everywhere else in England: and by destructive inclosures beggars and depopulates the country.

William Stukeley on the Avenue, *Stonehenge* (1740), 35

LIST OF ILLUSTRATIONS

ACKNOWLEDGEMENTS

The Commissioners wish to acknowledge the good work of their executive staff in the preparation of this report. It is substantially the work of Mr D.J. Bonney and Dr I.F. Smith. Mr H.C. Bowen has provided advice at all stages. Mr A.L. Pope did the drawings with assistance from Mr P.A. Spencers, who also designed the cover. Air photography and other photographic work was carried out by Mr R.E.W. Parsons, Mr J. Parkinson and Mr D. Kendall; special photographic sorties were flown by the National Monuments Record under the guidance of Mr J.N. Hampton. Mrs C. Stoertze helped with transcription work from air photographs. Mr H.G. Welfare, Mrs G.K. Popper and Mrs M. Thompson assisted with the editorial work.

The Commissioners are grateful to the following for generous assistance in the compilation of this survey: Mr A.J. Clark (Ancient Monuments Laboratory, DOE); Major H.L. Vatcher and the late Mrs Faith Vatcher (Avebury Museum); Dr J. Chandler (Amesbury Public Library); the Committee for Aerial Photography, University of Cambridge; the Archaeology Branch, Ordnance Survey; the staffs of Devizes Museum and Salisbury and South Wiltshire Museum; the staff of the County Record Office, Trowbridge; and the several landowners and tenants who readily allowed access to their land, in particular the National Trust and its tenants in the 1400 acres around Stonehenge.

Photographs are reproduced with the permission of the following individuals and institutions, in whom copyright is vested: Plates 2, 9 Ashmolean Museum, Oxford (Allen Collection); 6b, 10, 15, 21 Committee for Aerial Photography, University of Cambridge; 7, 23, iv West Air Photography, Weston-super-Mare; iii Meridian Airmaps Ltd; 8, 16 Mr P. Goodhugh; 18 Mr J. Hancock; 22 Ordnance Survey (Crown Copyright); endpaper, Salisbury and S. Wilts Museum. Plates 3, 11, 12, 13, 14, 17, 20, i, ii are from photographs in possession of the National Monuments Record (Crown Copyright).

FOREWORD

This publication is the outcome of a new review of the field monuments in a select area of about thirteen square miles around Stonehenge. The archaeological importance of this area has relevance far beyond even our national boundaries and the Commissioners consider that they should provide an up-to-date evaluation of the monuments within it to coincide with the issue of the Report on the future of Stonehenge anticipated from the Working Party set up by the Secretary of State for the Environment in July 1977.

The book is to be regarded as one of the Commission's *Occasional Publications*. The title is a deliberate choice. It is that given by Sir Richard Colt Hoare to his map of the antiquities around Stonehenge, the first reliable archaeological exposition of the area in cartographic form, made in the early years of the nineteenth century and an essential starting point for any subsequent review.

Care has been taken not to duplicate the thorough account of barrows already published elsewhere; only additional information is included here. Since an awareness of former land use in all its variety is the best way of understanding the pattern and condition of monuments left to us, very special attention has been paid to this aspect. A short section is directed to general recommendations for conservation with particular reference to those monuments which come within the ambit of any development close to Stonehenge itself. A number of specific subjects are also suggested as worthy of further investigation.

ADEANE
Chairman

COMMISSIONERS

The Right Honourable the Lord Adeane, PC, GCB, GCVO (*Chairman*)
Her Majesty's Lieutenant of the County of Wiltshire (*ex officio*)
Sheppard Sunderland Frere, Esq.
Richard John Copland Atkinson, Esq.
George Zarnecki, Esq., CBE
John Kenneth Sinclair St Joseph, Esq., CBE
Paul Ashbee, Esq.
Arthur Richard Dufty, Esq., CBE
Mark Girouard, Esq.
Christopher Nugent Lawrence Brooke, Esq.
Andrew Colin Renfrew, Esq.
Irene Joan Thirsk
Peter Kidson, Esq.
Maurice Warwick Beresford, Esq.
Robert Angus Buchanan, Esq.
Albert Lionel Frederick Rivet, Esq.

Secretary
Peter Jon Fowler, Esq.

EDITORIAL NOTES

For a recent review of the prehistory and early history of the county within which Stonehenge lies the reader is referred to VCH *Wilts* I (ii).

Barrows. The barrows of Wiltshire were first comprehensively listed by number and parish over fifty years ago (Goddard 1913). L.V.Grinsell revised and extended Goddard's work, using the same system of numbering, in his List of Wiltshire Barrows in VCH *Wilts* I (i). This remains the definitive list. The barrows recorded in the inventory below are, with the exception of a few amendments, additional to that list and almost entirely the product of aerial photography. A comprehensive list of barrow excavations is given in VCH *Wilts* I (i). Only excavations undertaken since that list was compiled (*c*.1951) are summarised in the inventory; many of them still await full publication.

Maps. All known monuments are shown on Map 1; those that survive substantially in relief are distinguished from those that have been levelled, or almost levelled, by ploughing and other destructive agencies. 'Celtic' fields are not so differentiated because even over small areas their condition varies widely.

All barrows are shown by type on Map 2; an attempt has been made to distinguish those that have been excavated or dug into, although surviving records do not permit complete accuracy.

Information about land use, shown on Map 3, is drawn largely from maps most of which are of eighteenth and nineteenth-century date. Information from documentary sources other than maps is too often unlocatable. The extent of old grassland in 1971 serves to emphasise the inroads of cultivation, especially on the downland, since *c*.1840.

Air Photographs. A large number of photographs exists of Stonehenge and the area around it. Many were taken between the two World Wars and they are now of considerable historical value, in particular those collected by the late O.G.S.Crawford while Archaeology Officer, Ordnance Survey, and now in the care of the National Monuments Record. Only the more informative photographs are quoted by number and a selection appear as illustrations.

National grid references. The prefix letters SU apply to all the grid references and for this reason the prefix has been omitted throughout.

Dates. In order to convert them to calendar years, dates derived from radiocarbon determinations have to be corrected to compensate for fluctuating levels of atmospheric radio-activity. Following standard practice, uncorrected radiocarbon dates are distinguished by the suffix 'bc' and followed by their laboratory numbers in brackets (*see* CBA *Radiocarbon Index*). This is because we cannot be certain that corrected ('calibrated') dates quoted currently will not, with more research, need adjustment. However, if Clark (1975) is followed, the calendar dates will generally be considerably earlier than the radiocarbon dates, though not in a constant ratio. Thus, in approximate figures, 2200 bc, the earliest date known for Stonehenge I, would become 2800 BC in terms of true chronology (*cf*. p.8) but a date of some 1000 bc would need a lesser correction, to perhaps 1250 BC.

THE MONUMENTS

'It is to be hoped that our grand-children will not have to look for Stonehenge in a field of turnips', wrote William Long in 1876. Fortunately his hope has been realised, but a century ago the threat to the monument and the antiquities around it was a very real one. Ploughing was in process of levelling, or had already levelled, many of the smaller, less obtrusive monuments in the area and it had caused very considerable damage even to some of the larger, such as Durrington Walls. The process, though somewhat subdued, continues. Despite this damage, intrusion of plantations, tarmacadam and barbed wire, and the activities of the Ministry of Defence, landscape around Stonehenge has in the course of the last few centuries changed less than most in Southern England. It still contains much that would be familiar to earlier generations of antiquaries, including Sir Richard Colt Hoare and his collaborator William Cunnington who explored its antiquities with such zeal in the early years of the nineteenth century, and William Stukeley who did likewise nearly a century earlier.

BARROWS AND CEREMONIAL MONUMENTS

The concentration of archaeological remains within the area around Stonehenge is remarkable, both in its density and in its composition, when compared with surrounding areas. Analysis shows that the monuments belong almost exclusively to the Neolithic and Bronze Ages; only about fifteen have been noted that do not certainly or probably belong to those periods, if it is accepted that the 'Celtic' fields and the boundary ditches are probably of the Bronze Age, at least in origin. The large number of round barrows, about four hundred, is especially striking and invites comparison with two other notable concentrations in Wessex, that around Avebury in North Wiltshire, and that along the Ridgeway in South East Dorset (RCHM 1970, iii, 420–80). Stonehenge was an important component of this concentration, and therefore largely responsible for much of it, but it was not, at least on existing evidence, the earliest. By analogy with other areas where radiocarbon dates are available it is fairly certain that the long barrows, the long mortuary enclosure on Normanton Down (dated by radiocarbon to 2560 bc ± 103 (BM-505)), and the two cursuses are all earlier than the first period at Stonehenge, for which a radiocarbon date of 2180 bc ± 105 (I-2328) exists. To these may be added the causewayed camp on Robin Hood's Ball, just to the N of the area under review.

It is undoubted, therefore, that Stonehenge was built in an area already notable in monuments; particularly the two cursuses, best regarded as ritual in purpose. This type of earthwork has not so far been found outside the British Isles. It is not clear, however, in what sense Stonehenge can be related to the earlier ceremonial tradition.

There are ten long barrows in the area, including two long since levelled by ploughing and only recently discovered by aerial photography (Amesbury 140; Winterbourne Stoke 71). The mounds vary in length from 20 m to 80 m, but the majority are between 30 m and 60 m, a modest size. All can be seen to have had side-ditches. Some have attracted later round barrows to them, notably Winterbourne Stoke (1) and Wilsford (41). The long mortuary enclosure is believed to be related to funerary practices associated with long barrows (possibly involving the exposure of corpses before interment) and perhaps specifically to the long barrow close by (Wilsford 30).

The cursuses were being built within the period of long barrow construction and it is significant that one of the biggest long barrows in the area (Amesbury 42) lies just beyond and parallel to the E end of the Stonehenge Cursus. The latter is nearly 3 km long, and the work involved in building such a monument argues for a compelling religious or ceremonial need as well as a high degree of social organisation. Even the Lesser Cursus is 400 m long.

These needs and capacities are reflected in the monuments which were built somewhat later. In the late Neolithic period appears a new kind of ceremonial monument, circular in form, which has been given by modern archaeologists the generic and misleading name of 'henge'. It is misleading because the term derives from 'Stonehenge' itself and almost certainly refers to the 'hanging' stones, the great uprights and lintels, that are found in no other henge monument and that appear late in the history of Stonehenge itself. It is also misleading because henge monuments almost always have ditches internal to their banks, as in other examples mentioned here and known elsewhere in Wessex, but that of Stonehenge is *external* to its bank. Its long period of development further marks out Stonehenge as unique among ceremonial monuments.

Durrington Walls, which has yielded a group of three radiocarbon dates around 2000 bc, is roughly contemporary with Stonehenge I. It is an enormous construction up to 490 m across overall, with a broad internal ditch over 5 m deep. The two structures excavated within this enclosure, represented by concentric timber settings, are probably temples or shrines; they are closely paralleled by the arrangement within the much smaller site of Woodhenge. A fourth henge, on Coneybury Hill, though totally flattened by ploughing and visible only on air photographs, appears to be even smaller than Woodhenge, and is oval rather than round. Its entrance points NE, like that of Stonehenge and Woodhenge, an orientation otherwise uncommon for henges with single entrances.

The position of the henges is of interest. Durrington Walls and Woodhenge lie close to the River Avon, and the former, by means of its SE entrance, appears to have a quite deliberate association with it. The henge on Coneybury Hill is set well above the river but within sight of Stonehenge. The latter appears to have had no particular association with water until a late stage in its use (when the Avenue was extended). The straight part of the Avenue, built on to Stonehenge in Period II, has produced radiocarbon dates of 1770 bc ± 100 (HAR-2013) and 1728 bc ± 68 (BM-1164).

By this time the custom of single burial, usually under a round barrow but sometimes in a flat grave, had been introduced by the Beaker people and was soon adopted widely by the native population. A number of Beaker burials in barrows have been found in the Stonehenge area including two (Durrington 65b and 67) near Woodhenge and Durrington Walls, two (Amesbury 51 and 54) near the W end of the Stonehenge Cursus, one (Winterbourne Stoke 35c) immediately W of the Lesser Cursus and three (Wilsford 51, 52 and 54) on Wilsford Down near the so-called 'North Kite' earthwork, itself perhaps of early Bronze Age date (p.26). An unusual Beaker flat grave was found in a small 'hengiform' enclosure in Fargo Plantation just S of the Cursus. In 1978 a burial of Beaker age, but without the characteristic pot, was discovered in the ditch surrounding Stonehenge.

After the Beaker period the rate of barrow building appears to have increased. It is unlikely that the small proportion of the population accorded barrow burial changed appreciably. A rising population may have been partly responsible, but it is also likely that the dead were brought from further afield than hitherto to be buried in an area of established religious importance. By this time the great ceremonial monuments had, with the exception of Stonehenge, fallen out of use. This main period of barrow building saw the creation of the great barrow groups. Bowl barrows continued to be built but, in addition, numerous barrows of new and more elaborate type, in particular bell barrows and disc barrows, made their appearance. Many of these comprised the memorials of a wealthy, and probably markedly hierarchal, society which, on the evidence of the objects buried with its individual members, enjoyed widespread trading contacts with Ireland, much of Europe and perhaps even the Mediterranean.

The barrows are sometimes grouped in relation to an earlier long barrow as, for example, in the Lake Group and at Longbarrow Cross Roads; and several of the groups are essentially linear cemeteries, involving arrangement along a ridge, notably the Normanton Group, the Cursus Group, in part the Wilsford Group and the Cross Roads Group itself. Most of the barrow groups, and many of the more scattered barrows, lie in prominent positions and in sight of Stonehenge, though today copses and plantations often hide them. The large group at Longbarrow Cross Roads, however, lies just out of sight.

Towards the middle of the second millennium BC this relatively short but intensive phase of specialised barrow building came to a fairly sudden end. Thereafter, during the remainder of the Bronze Age, the area assumes a less wealthy aspect. Its inhabitants appear to have been involved far less in trade and to an increasing extent in farming. It is probably within this period that many of the areas under 'Celtic' fields were cultivated on a more regular basis or brought into cultivation for the first time and that many of the boundary earthworks, both associated with and superseding the fields, were constructed. The Wilsford shaft (p.19), sunk to a depth of some 30 m, is a remarkable and enigmatic monument of the Middle Bronze Age.

Plate 2. WINTERBOURNE STOKE Cross Roads Barrow Group, from the south: land use in the 1930s

Plate 3. WINTERBOURNE STOKE Cross Roads Barrow Group, from the north: land use in 1976

SETTLEMENTS AND ENCLOSURES

Occupation sites of a number of periods occur in the vicinity of Stonehenge but their numbers are inevitably small in such a limited area. Almost without exception they have been heavily ploughed.

Remains of earlier Neolithic settlement are confined to pottery and other occupation debris preserved beneath or within later monuments. Such material has been found beneath the bank of Durrington Walls, there dated to the later fourth millennium BC (p.17), and beneath the bank of Woodhenge (p.19). Comparable pottery is known from a nearby barrow (Durrington 70; sherds in Devizes Museum) and from the fill of a flat grave at Totterdown, Amesbury (p.7). Further finds (see 'Barrow Excavations') come from two barrows E of Stonehenge (Amesbury 39 and 132) and from three barrows E of Lake Wood (Wilsford 51, 52, 54). Traces of later Neolithic occupation, all accompanied by Grooved Ware, have been found beneath the banks of both Durrington Walls and Woodhenge, at several sites near these monuments and also elsewhere in the parishes of Amesbury and Durrington. Contemporary material is also known from a number of barrows in Wilsford (36f, 37–9, 51, 52, 54, see 'Barrow Excavations'). Attention may also be drawn to the large quantities of worked flints collected from 'King Barrow Ridge' (centred 135426; Laidler and Young 1938; additional finds, some attributed to 'Avenue Field', are in the museums at Salisbury, Devizes and Avebury). A similar collection comes from the area around the former Starveall Plantation (121404; unpublished, in Devizes Museum).

Middle Bronze Age occupation has been identified S of Woodhenge and at Longbarrow Cross Roads, Winterbourne Stoke. The former site (p.23), partly excavated by Cunnington (1929), comprised a small egg-shaped enclosure, apparently used for stock, linked to a form of boundary ditch. Air photographs taken during the drought of 1976 have revealed further features; a complex of ditches forming rectangular enclosures of at least two phases is linked in part to the 'egg' enclosure. A broad ditched trackway approaches the enclosures from the north. Several finds of occupation debris in the immediate vicinity are probably indicative of contemporary domestic sites. The settlement at Longbarrow Cross Roads (p.22) has produced evidence of what were probably circular houses. It appears to be associated with one or more enclosures, with a number of boundary ditches, one of which extends for over 4 km, and possibly with 'Celtic' fields. The small enclosures associated with boundary earthworks and 'Celtic' fields on Rox Hill (p.24) and SW of Fargo Plantation (p.24) are undated and require further investigation, but a Bronze Age date is a strong possibility.

The few known Iron Age or Romano-British occupation sites within the Stonehenge area suggest a density below that for South Wiltshire as a whole. The hill-fort of Vespasian's Camp is the only visible Iron Age monument; its substantial defences, modified by eighteenth-century landscaping and cloaked with trees, enclose some 15 ha (37 acres) of a strongly defensive site within a bend of the River Avon (p.20). Little is known of its history. During the medieval period and after, the interior formed part of the unenclosed arable of West Amesbury known as Walls Field, and it was heavily ploughed until landscaping put an end to cultivation. Further N a small four-sided enclosure, totally levelled by ploughing, was found at the E end of the Packway in Durrington and partly excavated. It proved to be of late Iron Age date but most of the interior had been severely eroded by the plough. Excavations also revealed Iron Age occupation within Durrington Walls and, just outside the monument to the SW, part of a Romano-British settlement, the main nucleus of which probably lay further W (p.24). A second Romano-British settlement is suggested by the presence of pottery on either side of Fargo Road and on the fringe of a group of 'Celtic' fields.

Of unknown date, but probably Romano-British or earlier, are the rectangular enclosure SW of Fargo Plantation (p.24) and the curvilinear enclosures N and E of Druid's Lodge in Berwick St James (p.22) and Woodford (p.25). Also undated are the angular enclosure N of Normanton (p.24) and the markedly rectangular enclosure on Winterbourne Stoke Down, though the latter suggests a medieval or later date.

BOUNDARY EARTHWORKS

A number of boundary earthworks are known in the area, most of them in the SW part. Where they survive in relief, usually in field boundaries or woodland, they normally comprise a single bank and ditch, and in their dimensions overall they vary from about 7 m across to as much as 14 m. Ploughing has taken its toll of such earthworks; most have been damaged or levelled in part, some have been completely levelled and are known only from air photographs. It is likely that most, perhaps all, of the boundaries originated in the Bronze Age, but little precise evidence is available. Excavation of the boundary immediately N of Stonehenge (p.25) has revealed evidence of a Bronze Age date, and a cutting across the bank of the so-called 'North Kite' earthwork on Wilsford Down (p.26) has shown that it was built over a soil containing pottery no later than the Early Bronze Age. The southern end of the W side of this earthwork appears to be earlier than two round barrows probably both of the Early Bronze Age. The Middle Bronze Age settlement at Longbarrow Cross Roads (p.26) adjoins a boundary; and on Rox Hill (p.26) and SW of Fargo Plantation (p.26) boundaries appear to be integrated with 'Celtic' fields and enclosures, probably parts of settlements. West and SW of The Diamond plantation (105408) boundaries lie over 'Celtic' fields, and N of Luxenborough Plantation (130415) a boundary ditch appears to bend to avoid round barrows.

Unusually narrow ditches (p.29), visible only on air photographs, form a partial enclosure around, but of later date than, the long barrow Wilsford (34). They appear to underlie the major boundary earthwork immediately to the west.

'CELTIC' FIELDS

No fields have survived completely undamaged by later cultivation or other activity; many have been reduced to low rounded scarps and others are so flattened that they are now detectable only from the air. Present ascertainable distribution of 'Celtic' fields is noticeably towards the west part of the area, on the margins of the various parishes, where they have survived in areas of former pasture that lay beyond the limits of intensive cultivation in the medieval period and after. The fields on Lake Down and Rox Hill are an exception because here the old pasture occupied a more easterly position within the parish. There can be little doubt that originally 'Celtic' fields were more extensive. It is also fairly certain, however, that in some areas they never existed, in particular immediately N, E and S of Stonehenge and over much of Normanton Down. These areas have not been heavily ploughed and, had fields once existed here, some evidence of their former presence might be expected to have survived.

No single orientation is discernible in the layout of the fields throughout the area as a whole or over any substantial part of it. Some consistency of alignment (ENE–WSW) may be detected in the two small groups of fields on Durrington Down and also in the fragmentary fields to be found NNE of Druid's Lodge, around 102400. Certain differences in alignment suggest that some blocks of fields were laid out independently of each other. In most cases there are no clear limits to the fields; they stop or peter out in areas where heavier subsequent ploughing has obliterated them. The group of fields SW of Fargo Plantation, however, does appear to end on the N at a continuous boundary lynchet. The sizes of individual fields vary widely and, because of the destructive activities of later ploughing, many are incomplete. Very few small square fields are present; a few with dimensions of about 35 m by 45 m occur in the group S of Fargo Plantation. In the same group, and also E of the plantation, are long narrow fields which may well have been enlarged in antiquity by the removal of internal divisions rather than originally laid out in this form. It is possible that some have been altered by relatively modern ploughing.

On general grounds 'Celtic' fields are known to have been in use by the earlier stages of the Bronze Age in the first half of the second millennium BC. There is no certain relationship between 'Celtic' fields and a Bronze Age settlement in the area but it is possible that the settlement at Longbarrow Cross Roads (p.22) is related to the fields just E of it. The enclosure on Rox Hill (120387; p.31) is integrated with a phase of the 'Celtic' fields around it, though perhaps not the earliest. Boundary earthworks overlie 'Celtic' fields W and S of The Diamond plantation at 103408, 102401, and possibly at 10654025. South of Fargo Plantation a boundary earthwork runs conformably through fields; and on Rox Hill (around 121388) a boundary makes sudden changes of direction apparently to conform to fields and appears, therefore, to be later.

Only one long barrow (Winterbourne Stoke 71) lies clearly among 'Celtic' fields but the latter bear no relation to its alignment. The ditched 'enclosure' (p.29) around, and possibly integrated with, the long barrow Wilsford (34) shares a common alignment with the 'Celtic' fields a short distance to the northwest. A number of round barrows, all levelled by ploughing, lie among 'Celtic' fields on the line of the lynchets and sometimes at the corners of fields, e.g. Durrington (8) and (38), Winterbourne Stoke (23a), (74) and (81), and Wilsford (101).

In addition to damage by modern ploughing, air photographs show that 'Celtic' fields have been modified and damaged in the past by ridge-and-furrow or strip cultivation, notably s of Longbarrow Cross Roads, Winterbourne Stoke and on Rox Hill, Wilsford cum Lake.

CONDITION OF THE MONUMENTS

The destructive and, more rarely, protective forces that have acted on monuments are discussed below. Here the general condition of field monuments today is summarised.

Barrows. Many round barrows and at least two long barrows (Amesbury 140 and Winterbourne Stoke 71) had been levelled by cultivation before such antiquaries as Stukeley (1740) and Hoare (1810) made their studies of the area. Most of the eighty barrows recorded below (pp. 1–4) come into this category; others have been levelled since accurate maps began to be made in the early nineteenth century. Although ploughing is still gradually levelling some barrows, legislation in the present century has done much to arrest further destruction; some of the finest surviving barrows, and also groups of barrows, are to be found in the vicinity of Stonehenge, several of them in plantations.

Cursuses and henges. Far more of the Stonehenge Cursus survives, though somewhat damaged, than is generally appreciated. The associated long barrow just beyond its E end is less fortunate; a modern track follows its spine and its E side is in arable. The Lesser Cursus, Woodhenge (now in the care of the DOE, the position of former wooden uprights marked by concrete drums) and the henge monument on Coneybury Hill have all been levelled by ploughing as has the eastern two-thirds of the Stonehenge Avenue. Cultivation has also finally removed much of the bank of the great henge at Durrington Walls.

Settlements and enclosures. Ploughing has flattened, or all but flattened, all the settlements and enclosures recorded below with the sole exception of the Iron Age hill-fort, Vespasian's Camp. The interior of the latter has been heavily ploughed, the ramparts slightly modified by landscaping and the whole planted with trees.

'Celtic' fields and boundary earthworks. Nearly all the known 'Celtic' fields are in arable and the lynchets defining them have in consequence been reduced or levelled. Some of the best preserved fields are on Durrington Down (around 121444) and N of Rox Hill (around 122389). The boundary earthworks have suffered similarly, whatever their proportions, and tend to survive only in woodland or where use has been made of them for later boundaries (parish, estate or field).

RECOMMENDATIONS FOR CONSERVATION

It is apparent that Stonehenge and the monuments in its environs constitute a remarkable concentration of sites. The whole area illustrated in our General Map is one of particular archaeological importance and should be designated an Archaeological Area (Ancient Monuments and Archaeological Areas Act, 1979) with critical attention paid to the proper management of the monuments. We wish especially to draw attention to the following in the more immediate area around Stonehenge:

The Stonehenge Cursus, a ceremonial precursor of Stonehenge, should be protected from any further degradation, and in addition its course through Fargo Plantation be cleared of scrub and, very carefully, of trees. The related *long barrow*, crossed by a track just E of the flattened E end, should be protected from further damage by diversion of the track; the area between it and the end of the Cursus should be cleared and protected.

Stonehenge Avenue, where it exists as an earthwork, should be protected from any wear that might damage its grass cover.

The barrow group immediately W of Stonehenge (Amesbury 4–10a), though much degraded, should be protected from further levelling and from any non-archaeological digging.

The barrows within the s end of Fargo Plantation should be cleared of scrub and trees as already recommended for the Cursus area.

Finally, it must be emphasised that all the ground close to the circle of Stonehenge itself is of the highest archaeological potential and has never been systematically explored. It is recommended therefore, that care should be taken to prevent any non-archaeological digging without the most careful prior consultation.

SUGGESTIONS FOR FURTHER INVESTIGATION

The processes of archaeological investigation and interpretation are of necessity, and desirability, continuing ones; the definitive statement is rare. Every monument and topic in the following pages is worthy of further study; in so many instances it has hardly begun.

There is a notable lack of palaeo-environmental information. Small soil pits sunk into gutted barrows, for instance, could produce useful results in an economical way. Evidence for settlements is also very slight. Systematic field walking is worth undertaking because, although it is certain that most occupation material on the surface will have been destroyed by plough and weather, it is possible that exceptional circumstances, especially new deep ploughing, may expose valuable evidence. Searches could also help to define the area of bluestone chippings more clearly than at present. Settlement evidence is needed to help date the 'Celtic' fields in the area, whose cultivation, especially s w of Stonehenge, could perhaps best explain wind-blown layers found by excavators at Stonehenge. Soil movement generally has been inadequately investigated. The examination of hill-wash deposits would be of particular interest in Stonehenge Bottom close to where it is crossed by the still visible Cursus and Avenue.

Some specific points for future work are suggested as follows:

(a) The geophysical examination of an area some 100 m in radial extent outside the Stonehenge earthwork in order to identify the presence of any buried structures responsive to such examination.

(b) Geophysical examination, and perhaps selective excavation, to see whether the 'gaps' in the Stonehenge Cursus mentioned by Stukeley and Hoare are original as they believed (p.14).

(c) Investigation of the E end of the Lesser Cursus and also of the cross-bank within it and its relationship to the monument as a whole (p.19).

(d) Completion of the geophysical survey of the interior of Durrington Walls.

(e) Geophysical survey accompanied by test excavation of the henge on Coneybury Hill (p.13).

(f) Further investigations of the 'North Kite' earthwork (p.26), in particular to confirm its date, at present believed to be Early Bronze Age, and its relationship to adjoining boundary earthworks.

(g) Test excavations to establish the relationship of the disc barrow (Wilsford 45b), and perhaps also of barrows (46) and (47), to the boundary earthwork in Lake Wood just s of the 'North Kite' (p.26).

(h) Investigation of the nature and date of the enclosures associated with boundary earthworks and 'Celtic' fields: (i) on Rox Hill at 120387 (p.24); (ii) south of Fargo Plantation at 109421 (p.22).

LAND USE

Two factors are of paramount importance to an understanding of the present condition and distribution of archaeological sites and monuments; (i) the differing capacities of archaeological sites to survive in the face of subsequent human activity and (ii) local differences in the intensity of that activity. Even within small areas the operation of these factors is clearly visible and the area around Stonehenge well illustrates this. It is rarely possible to document the destructive processes in any detail, unless they are of relatively recent origin, but it is abundantly clear that such processes are in no way limited to the present century as is often believed. Around Stonehenge the requirements of agriculture, particularly of the plough, have been by far the most destructive force over the centuries; but other developments have damaged monuments and, more rarely and probably inadvertently, contributed to their survival.

ARABLE FARMING AND ITS ENCROACHMENT ON THE DOWNLAND

There is already some evidence that even in antiquity the activities of men were modifying or obliterating the works of their predecessors. Such evidence is often revealed by the surface remains of field monuments, and very frequently in excavations on archaeological sites. Here some attempt is made to view the subject in terms of the more obvious recent historical sources, in particular, maps.

Throughout the medieval period and long after, a recurring and almost ubiquitous pattern of land use is to be found in the parishes, estates and manors of the Wessex chalklands within which the Stonehenge area lies. Settlements lay along the rivers and streams, usually on the gravel terraces flanking them, with ready access to water, essential in this dry landscape. The land associated with each of these settlements and worked by its inhabitants usually took the form of a strip of varying length and width which extended from the valley bottom to the top of a ridge or other high ground. The existing pattern of parishes to some extent reflects this arrangement but it is only fully revealed when the individual tithings or manors comprising the parishes are also plotted (e.g. Bonney 1976).

In this way each settlement had access to a cross-section of the agricultural potential of the area generally. The wet meadows occupied the valley bottom, the permanent arable of the open-fields usually the lower slopes, and pasture the higher remoter lands and steep uncultivable slopes. The arable was by no means immutably fixed and from time to time areas of downland were taken into temporary cultivation and returned again to pasture. From the seventeenth century onwards this was often achieved by burn-baking, i.e. paring and burning the surface before ploughing.

Cultivation appears to have been making substantial inroads on the downland in Wiltshire by the early eighteenth century when Defoe (1928, i, 285), in writing of the upland sheep pastures, noted that 'so much of these downs are plowed up, as has increased the quantity of corn produced in this county, in a prodigious manner, and lessened their quantity of wooll'. From the later eighteenth century onwards parliamentary inclosure brought an end to communal, open-field farming with its necessary, but sometimes constricting, regulations and replaced it with ring-fenced farming. The latter permitted a freer and more flexible use of agricultural land and almost certainly contributed to the ploughing-up of much traditional pasture often with dire consequences for any earthworks therein.

The impact of cultivation on monuments in the Stonehenge area inevitably varies from parish to parish as also does the quantity of documentary and other evidence relating to it. Relevant information is therefore presented by parish.

Amesbury

The documentary evidence relating to cultivation is far better for Amesbury than for any of the other parishes in the Stonehenge area. The parish is a large one, straddling the River Avon; but here only the part w of the river is relevant. It was divided between two settlements, Amesbury Countess on the N and West Amesbury on the s, and their lands extended from the river westwards to the parish boundary with Winterbourne Stoke. The great bell barrow (Amesbury 55), known as Goars Barrow in 1639 (WRO 283/4), traditionally marked the division between the two at that boundary. The open-fields of the two settlements adjoined and occupied most of the parish between the river on the E and the Seven Barrows ridge, and the w side of Coneybury Hill on the west. Cultivation within this area was intensive; even the interior of the Iron Age hill-fort, Vespasian's Camp, was under the plough by the late fourteenth century and probably much earlier. Few earthworks survived this and it is significant that neither Hoare, nor Stukeley before him, saw much to record E of Seven Barrows. Hoare's map (Pl. 1) shows only three barrows (38a, 39b and c) here, and these survive as earthworks today.

Air photography, however, has revealed numerous flattened earthworks, especially round barrows/ring-ditches, and there would seem little reason to doubt that all these had been effectively flattened by the time Stukeley made his study of the area in 1719–24, and probably much earlier. The Stonehenge Avenue is the most striking example. Stukeley was unable to trace it for more than about 90 m E of the top of the Seven Barrows ridge (Pl. 4) and beyond that point could only guess (incorrectly) at its real course. It has been left to air photography to establish its true line (Pls. 8 and 9). Further s, ploughing within the open-fields of West Amesbury has completely levelled a small henge monument, several barrows and a boundary ditch.

West of the open-fields lay the open down, traditionally the sheep pasture, but by the eighteenth century small portions of it were being broken up, if only on a temporary basis. A document of 1734 (WRO 283/142) relating to land in The Homeward Farm, West Amesbury, mentions 'Part of Stonehenge to be ploughed 20 a[cres]' (8 ha). Temporary ploughing of this kind might well account for the denuded condition of the prehistoric boundary earthwork which crosses the down immediately N of Stonehenge (p.25). A survey (WRO 944/3) of 1771 mentions under Countess Court Farm two areas of 'Plough'd Down, now in Grass': part of Countess Court Down, twenty-two acres (9 ha) and part of Little Amesbury Cow Down, nearly thirty-two acres (13 ha). The latter is almost certainly part of what is now Fargo Plantation. A map and sale particulars of 1823 (WRO 283/202) show that the area later occupied by the

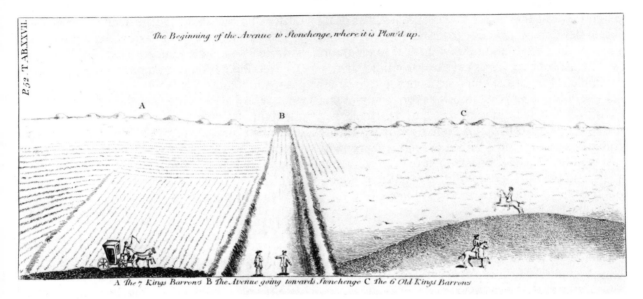

Plate 4. STONEHENGE AVENUE east of the King Barrows in process of destruction by the plough, *after* Stukeley (1740, Tab. XXVII)

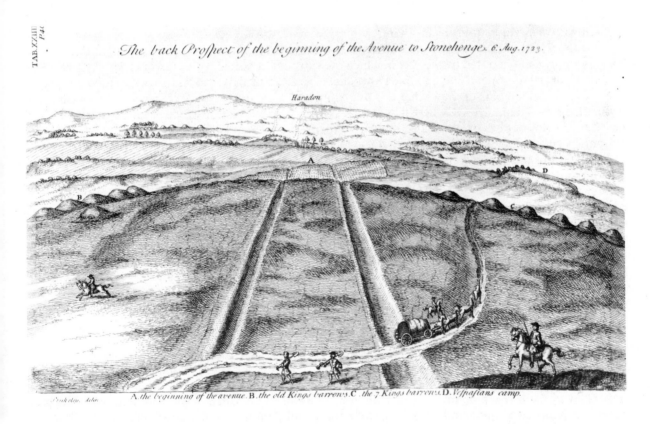

Plate 5. STONEHENGE AVENUE west of the King Barrows cut by the Amesbury to Market Lavington road, *after* Stukeley (1740, Tab. XXIV). Looking east.

plantation was then in arable, and regarded as part of Little Amesbury Cow Down. That this was not a recent development is clear from Hoare (1810, 163) who records that the bowl barrow Amesbury (54), just s of the Cursus and now within Fargo Plantation, had been 'some years under tillage'. Also in 1823 40 ha (just over 100 acres) of the down immediately s of Fargo Plantation and adjoining the A344 were in arable. More of the Cursus was brought under the plough in about 1850 when the remainder of the slope E of Stonehenge Bottom was broken up (Long 1876, 236).

In 1847 a small farm known as Fargo Cottages was built about 550 m w of Stonehenge and cultivation around it 'levelled two barrow-like mounds, which were in great measure formed of the chippings and fragments of the stones of Stonehenge' (Long 1876, 65n). The group of barrows, Amesbury (4–10a), just w of Stonehenge appears to have been deliberately reduced in height to facilitate ploughing in about 1848; and the small group to the sw of these, Amesbury (1–3) and (107–11), had by 1876 been 'nearly obliterated by a farmer, who has ploughed up this part of the down nearly to the stone circles' (*ibid.*, 236, 198n).

Wilsford cum Lake

The large number of extant barrows in the w half of the parish prompts speculation that many more might have been levelled, as in Amesbury, in the more intensively cultivated E part of the parish. This would appear not to be the case, however; air photography has so far revealed relatively few barrows or other earthworks here.

An unusual arrangement of arable and pasture existed in the manor of Lake which comprised the s part of the parish. The permanent pasture, Lake Down, lay centrally within the manor where a steep-sided combe acted as a deterrent to regular cultivation. Here prehistoric boundary banks and ditches, a notable barrow group and 'Celtic' fields have survived in old pasture (Pl. 18), but much of this has recently been brought under the plough. The arable lay on more level ground to the SE and NW of the down. The West Field was probably the largest single area of open-field arable within the manor but it is not known when cultivation began there. A map of Asserton (WRO 1553) shows that 'Lake Fields' abutted the parish of Berwick St James in 1655. The destructive nature of protracted cultivation in West Field is amply demonstrated by the way in which the substantial boundary earthworks, so well preserved on either side in Lake Wood and on Lake Down, have been totally flattened and are now visible only from the air. Hoare's map (Pl. 1) shows that this flattening had occurred by the early nineteenth century.

On the s side of Lake Down, where it rises to Rox Hill, strip cultivation of medieval or later date overlies 'Celtic' fields but has by no means obliterated them. It presumably represents one or more phases of temporary cultivation of the down but no documentary evidence has so far been found in support of this.

The N part of the parish comprises Normanton Farm which includes within it, and gives its name to, one of the most celebrated groups of barrows in the whole of Wessex. The Tithe Map (c.1838) shows a greater proportion of pasture to arable than elsewhere in the parish, probably a reflection of the small population here during and since the medieval period (VCH *Wilts* IV, 297, 306) and the consequent lack of pressure on land. There is, however, some evidence for cultivation of the down. Hoare (1810, 126) recorded that three of the group of small bowl barrows (Wilsford 11a–d) had been ploughed over and that as a consequence 'we gave up our researches, as, owing to the slight elevation of these barrows above the level of the ground, their contents would most probably have been destroyed by the continued operations of agriculture'. He also noted (*ibid.*, 207) that one of the barrows of the Normanton Group, probably Wilsford (29), 'is only the base of a large circular barrow, the earth having been removed for agricultural purposes'.

Durrington

The E part of the parish nearest the village was in open-field arable and the name Durrington Field, still current on OS maps, testifies to this. The impact of intensive cultivation on a major earthwork is well illustrated by the henge monument of Durrington Walls (Pl. 13). Much of its encircling bank has been effectively removed, its ditch infilled and almost entirely obliterated as a surface feature, and on the s side ploughing has given a spurious shape to the monument. Within a short distance to the s, cultivation has completely levelled a second but much smaller henge, Woodhenge, a number of round barrows, a Bronze

Age enclosure and a complex of ditches adjoining it (Pls. 14 and 16).

No early map of Durrington exists and the western limit of the open-fields is first recorded on the Inclosure Map of 1823. An agreement of 1740 'to burn, break up 12 acres [5 ha] of Down adjoining Shrewton Down' (Rev. Ruddle's Book, Durrington Vicarage) suggests that sporadic cultivation of the down remote from the village was taking place. The Tithe Map (1839) shows an irregular field adjoining the s boundary of the parish, beyond the limit of the former open-fields, known as the Burnbake, a name which implies temporary or intermittent cultivation. It was at that time in arable. A number of barrows lay within the Burnbake and Hoare (1810, 167) notes that one (Durrington 25) has been ploughed over and that two others (32 and 33) were 'in tillage'.

Berwick St James
Only the e tip of the parish, represented by part of the manor of Asserton, extends into the area. A map of the manor dated 1655 (WRO 1553) shows that most of this was downland but that it included a small area of arable, part of the East or Higher Field. The now totally flattened, and hitherto unrecorded, pre-historic or Romano-British enclosure at 097392 lies just within this former open-field, a fact which probably explains its obliteration.

The Tithe Map (c.1841) names the whole of the area e of the Salisbury-Devizes road as the Burnbake, and shows some of it in arable but the greater part in pasture. This probably reflects the intermittent nature of cultivation here, as its name implies.

Winterbourne Stoke
Only the e extremity of the parish lies within the area. The Tithe Map (c.1840) shows no arable here, but on air photographs (e.g. Pl. 22) there is clear evidence of ridge-and-furrow in furlongs s of Long-barrow Cross Roads. This represents medieval or post-medieval cultivation of the down and it appears to have been of sufficient intensity to obliterate in part the underlying 'Celtic' fields. At least one of the furlongs is crossed by the present Salisbury-Devizes road (A360) which was turnpiked soon after 1760 (VCH Wilts IV, 261–2). This implies that the road formerly followed a different line, possibly somewhat to the e, before converging at the cross roads. The various phases of ploughing have totally flattened a long barrow at 101409 (Winterbourne Stoke 71).

PLANTATIONS, COPSES AND EMPARKING
A number of plantations and copses laid out for ornamental purposes, for game coverts and for shelter belts contain earthworks, the condition of which is often dramatically better than that of their counter-parts in open country. There can be little doubt that the presence of the trees has protected the earthworks, albeit fortuitously, from the depredations of ploughing; but it is likely that some plantations were laid out in those very areas where substantial earthworks, especially compact groups of barrows, made plough-ing a difficult and unattractive proposition in an age without the tractor and the bulldozer. Most of the plantations are of relatively recent origin (post 1800) as the names of some imply, e.g. The Diamond and Starveall in Wilsford cum Lake, and Fargo at the western extremity of Amesbury parish.

The Wilsford Barrow Group provides one of the most striking examples of the way in which earth-works have survived in woodland and not outside it. In addition, it emphasises the vulnerability of disc barrows to ploughing (Pl. 6). The Wilsford Tithe Map shows the whole group within arable in 1851 but the comparable map for the adjacent tithing of Lake, undated but probably of similar or slightly earlier date, suggests that the plantation which now incorporates many of the barrows was already in existence. To the NW a small plantation, sometimes known as Lake Wood and also first recorded in 1848, has helped to protect many of the barrows of the Lake Group and portions of prehistoric boundary earthworks which lie within it (Fig. 15). Starveall Plantation (121404) was relatively short-lived; it first appears on OS 6-inch 1st ed. surveyed 1879, and had gone by 1957, but it has probably contributed to the survival of two barrows (Wilsford 55 and 56) as earthworks while others nearby are totally flattened. The area was arable in 1851 (Tithe Map) and is so once more. Normanton Gorse (114414), first recorded on the Tithe Map for Durnford (c.1838) and at that time known as Furze Cover, incorporates the only surviving portion of a boundary earthwork and also a remarkably well preserved disc barrow (Wilsford 2).

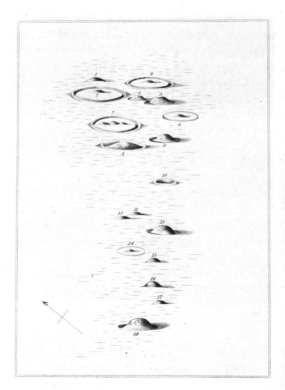

Plate 6. The WILSFORD Barrow Group. (a) *After* Hoare (1810, opp. 207), from the west. (b) In 1972, from the southeast; most of the group survives in wood

In Amesbury parish a number of plantations contain earthworks and, with the exception of those associated with Amesbury Park (*see* below), their first recorded appearance is on the Tithe Map (1846). Luxenborough Plantation, laid out just within the margins of the former open-fields of West Amesbury, includes two barrows, the best surviving examples of a small group. Other barrows survive as earthworks in unnamed plantations to the W (126415) and N (129418). Fargo Plantation is something of an exception. It had been in arable for some time before planting (p.xvi) and in consequence some of the earthworks within it, especially part of the Stonehenge Cursus, are not particularly well preserved.

The major emparking scheme within the area is that associated with Amesbury House. In 1725 the 3rd Duke of Queensberry succeeded to the House and its attendant estate and soon put in hand a programme of improvement which was to continue virtually until his death in 1778. This included the extension of the then existing park which, in a survey of 1726 by Henry Flitcroft (WRO944/1, 2), may be seen to have comprised some 12 ha (30 acres) surrounding the house and entirely on the E bank of the river. Charles Bridgeman, the Royal Gardener, was engaged from *c.*1730 on the improvement and enlargement of the park but his only surviving drawing of work there (Bodleian Gough Drawings a3) is dated 1738, the year in which he died, perhaps leaving the commission unfinished. It shows E of the river a larger, more elaborate park than that portrayed by Flitcroft with landscaping of the slope W of the river including part of the Iron Age hill-fort, Vespasian's Camp, above it (p.20). Andrews and Dury's Map (1773) confirms, insofar as its scale permits, that this scheme was followed fairly closely. This extension of the park, known as the Pleasure Ground, was largely planted with trees but incorporated walks and vistas (WRO 944/3; 283/202).

Andrews and Dury's Map also shows that by 1773 the park had been enlarged still further on the W and N to encompass a total of about 120 ha (300 acres). It comprised all the land N of the road from Amesbury towards Stonehenge as far W as, and including, the New King Barrows, and it extended almost as far as the Amesbury-Durrington road on the northeast. Much of this final extension was taken from the open-fields of West Amesbury and Amesbury Countess in or about 1765. In that year the estate accounts record expenditure on 'banking up the new pailing by the road from West Amesbury to the 7 Burrows [i.e. the New King Barrows]' (WRO 283/168). It was probably at about this time that the Old and New King Barrows were planted with the Scots firs which subsequently impeded the archaeological investigations of Cunnington and Hoare (1810, 157). The presence of these trees, together with the later addition of beeches, has undoubtedly protected the New King Barrows and contributed to their present remarkable condition. A field-book of 1771 (WRO 944/3) indicates that the whole of the enlarged park beyond the Pleasure Ground was laid to pasture, but it had probably been returned to arable before or at the death of the 3rd Duke. In 1781, under his successor, an order was given for the Park pale to be taken down (WRO 283/189). The Park was still a named and identifiable entity, though in arable, in 1823 (WRO 283/202), but by 1846 (Amesbury Tithe Map) only the plantations remained of the larger park.

The scatter of circular and oval tree-clumps which extends from N of Vespasian's Camp westwards to the King Barrows is popularly believed to represent the disposition of ships at either the Battle of the Nile (1798) or, less commonly, the Battle of Trafalgar. Though perhaps true, no reliable documentary evidence has emerged so far in support of this contention. The date of planting is unknown but the clumps are not shown on the Tithe Map and first appear unequivocally on OS 6-inch 1st ed. (surveyed 1879).

PENNINGS AND SHEEP FOLDS

The term 'penning' was used on the chalk downland primarily of an enclosure for sheep; but it appears also to have given its name to the area, often a dry valley bottom, in which such an enclosure was sited or even to later farm buildings put up nearby. Merewether (1851, 109–10) observed that '*The Pennings* is a term at present applied, as the cursory observer would suppose, to a farm-yard and fold near at hand; but the phrase belongs to a disused enclosure adjoining, of a double square in form, and of some extent, surrounded by a slight ditch and mound, on which still grow many stunted whitethorn bushes. The term *Pennings* is applied by the husbandmen to other similar enclosures and earthworks.' It would appear from this that the original pennings were already obsolete, or in process of becoming so, by the mid nineteenth century probably as the result of inclosure. Hoare (1810, 198) appears to have had difficulty in locating West Amesbury Penning mentioned by Aubrey. This lay near 127413 in Penning Bottom but there is no trace of an enclosure either on the ground or on air photographs. It was at or near this penning that Aubrey noted that the earthwork known as Normanton-ditch had been cut through in many places by the shepherds in pitching their fold (p.32). Shepherds, too, constructed a small fold on the SW side of Bush Barrow (Title page) and in the process cut a platform still visible; they also planted as a shelter the thorn bushes which led Stukeley (1740, 45) to give the barrow its name and the remnants of which are still prominent today (Pl. 20).

RABBITS

The destructive activities of rabbits, before their numbers were drastically reduced by myxomatosis from about 1950 onwards, are well known to field archaeologists. Earthworks and especially the fillings of their ditches, have always been attractive to rabbits because they provide them with an easier and often drier medium than the bedrock in which to dig burrows. Photographs, especially those taken from the air between the two World Wars, show extensive bald patches caused by rabbits on and around earthworks, and abandoned burrows are frequently found in excavations of barrows and other monuments.

In the medieval period, and indeed up to the present century, rabbits constituted an important source of meat and were often kept of set purpose in conigers and warrens, living larders akin to dovecotes and deer parks. These sometimes included earthworks, especially barrows, which the rabbits had already colonised or were imported so to do. The Coniger, an earthwork enclosure at Winterbourne Stoke (077420) first recorded by name in 1574, incorporates a number of Bronze Age round barrows, many of them badly damaged by rabbits. A notable example of the planned introduction of rabbits to barrows occurred in the early seventeenth century at Amesbury Abbey, then in the possession of the Earl of Hertford. A document of 1609/10 (WRO 283/6) records that in 1605 'Two round connye berryes were made to his Lordship's appointment and at the same time 14 couple of conies put into the ground. Which 14 couple of cunnies with theire encrease did breade and feed there. . . .'

The presence and activities of rabbits are referred to intermittently in records relating to Stonehenge and the area around it. Stukeley (1740, 32) noted that 'In 1724, when I was there, Richard Hayns an old man of Ambresbury, whom I employed to dig for me in the barrows, found some little worn-out Roman coins at Stonehenge, among the earth rooted up by the rabbets' (he also suspected that Hayns had planted the coins for reward). That the rabbits were a recognised warren and of some value is suggested in a lease of 1727/8 (WRO 282/132) in which certain items were reserved to the owner, Mr Hayward of West Amesbury, including 'The Rabbitt Burrows on West Hill and at Stonehenge'. Significantly West Hill is now known as Coneybury Hill (around 135414); it is surmounted by two round barrows. That the activities of the rabbits at Stonehenge were causing damage is clear from an entry in Stukeley's Diary (Vol. x, 4) for 12th December 1750, in which he records that the Duke of Queensberry, then owner of the monument, 'says he has taken great pains to destroy the rabbits which Mr Hayward, the former possessor, had planted there, on purpose to preserve this most noble antiquity' (Stukeley, *Diary* 274).

It seems likely that the Stonehenge rabbits also used, or spread to, the group of barrows (Amesbury 4–10a) just SW of the monument; Hoare (1810, 127) recorded that they were 'much defaced by rabbits'. Between 1761 and 1777 entries in the Amesbury Estate records (WRO 283/168) suggest that the rabbits in West Amesbury were regarded as a nuisance and that steps were being taken to eliminate or, at least, reduce them. Rabbits appear to have remained active at Stonehenge, however, and in 1863 the under-gamekeeper of Sir Edmund Antrobus is recorded as digging deeply for them in the vicinity of the fallen trilithon (Long 1876, 118). The latter fell in 1797 and it is difficult to resist the speculation that the activities of the rabbits, and of those who sought to breed them or eliminate them, contributed to its fall. In fairness to the rabbits, however, it must be added that human curiosity also played its part. Aubrey records (*ibid.*, 83) that in 1620 the Duke of Buckingham, in pursuing his researches into the monument 'did cause the middle of Stonehenge to be digged, and this under-digging was the cause of the falling downe, or recumbency of the great stone there, twenty one foote long.'

ROADS AND TRACKS

Certain roads and tracks have been realigned or have been entirely abandoned in the vicinity of Stonehenge but they have usually left behind some evidence of their former existence. It is clear from Andrews and Dury's map (1773), which antedates parliamentary inclosure in the area, that numerous roads crossed the unenclosed downland and that many of these have ceased to exist. These tracks, which were constricted by the arable fields around the villages, often spread out on reaching the open downland giving rise in places to a veritable network.

One of the best documented instances in the area of the realignment of a road concerns that from Amesbury to Market Lavington. On leaving Amesbury the road, as today, passes across the S part of the Iron Age hill-fort of Vespasian's Camp, a line at least as early as the fourteenth century (p.22). At the point where it now curves W and is joined by the present Amesbury by-pass, it formerly continued NW to turn and pass between the northernmost pair of the New King Barrows. This part of its course appears frequently as a crop or soil-mark on air photographs. It continued westward down the slope and in Stonehenge Bottom crossed the Avenue (Pl. 5) 'here much obscured by the wheels of carriages going over it, for a great way together' (Stukeley 1740, 35). After a short distance it also crossed the Cursus and then continued NW across Durrington Down. The enlargement of the Duke of Queensberry's park (p.xx) as far W as the New King Barrows in the mid eighteenth century necessitated a realignment of this road to avoid the SW corner of the park. A new road was laid out running NW from the corner of the park but it was apparently never completed (p.31). Two portions survive as earthworks in a remarkably straight line pointing directly at the corner of the park (Pl. 23). Considerable care was taken of the gradient by raising the road on a causeway where it crossed Stonehenge Bottom. The road was built across the Stonehenge Avenue and across part of the large bell barrow, Amesbury (43), but there is no evidence to suggest that an attempt was made to cross or breach the Cursus just to the NW of the barrow.

A track or road is known to have followed the line of the Avenue from Stonehenge as far as the bend in Stonehenge Bottom, where it crossed and flattened the bank and ditch, and then continued NE towards Durrington. A definite hollow along the NW side of the Avenue marks the line of this track. The earthworks of the eighteenth-century road blocked it, but its line appears to have been re-established by later

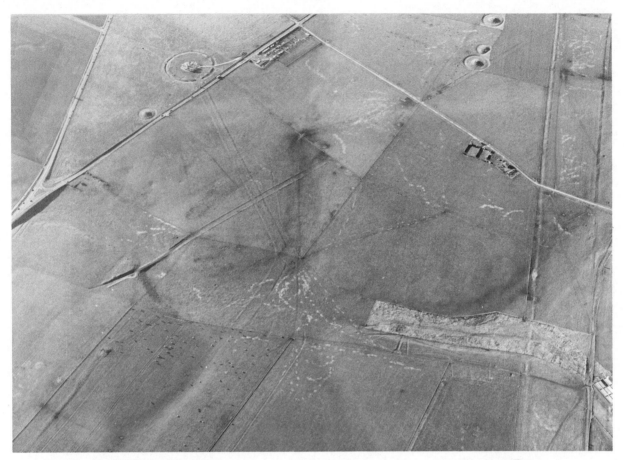

Plate 7. STONEHENGE from the NE showing the Avenue and 18th-century road: the Cursus on right of picture. 1977

use. The wear caused by this track at the bend in the Avenue was partly responsible for Stukeley's mistaken belief that the Avenue divided into two branches at this point.

A relatively modern road, and an unfortunate intrusion upon Stonehenge, is the A344 from Amesbury to Shrewton which passes close to the N side of the monument and also cuts the Avenue. It is almost certainly a creation of the early 1760s when most of the roads in the area were turnpiked and its very straight alignment supports such a view. There is no evidence to suggest that it existed before this. Stukeley's views (1740, Tab. III and XXVIII) do not show it and it is clear from Ogilby (1675, pl. 32) that in the later seventeenth century the road passed some considerable distance N of Stonehenge, leaving the Lavington road at the King Barrows and rejoining the present Shrewton road probably at the bend by Fargo Plantation.

South of Longbarrow Cross Roads in Winterbourne Stoke air photographs (Pl. 22) show clearly that the present Salisbury-Devizes road (A360), turnpiked soon after 1760, lies unconformably across a furlong of ridge-and-furrow of medieval or, more probably, later date (around 100408). At the time of ploughing this road either followed a more wandering course or did not exist. The characteristic hollowing of unmetalled roads and their habit of splaying, usually to avoid poorly drained, muddy sections, may be seen on early air photographs especially at Longbarrow Cross Roads (100414) and at the descent of A303 into Stonehenge Bottom.

MILITARY RAILWAYS AND OTHER INSTALLATIONS

In 1901 the London and South Western Railway constructed a branch line to Amesbury from Allington Junction on the main Waterloo-Salisbury line and extended it as far as Bulford in 1906. A proposal to build a line from Amesbury to Shrewton failed to materialise but shortly after the outbreak of the First

World War a light military railway was built to Larkhill leaving the Amesbury-Bulford line at Ratfyn Junction (162425). Further branches were built to the Balloon School at Rollestone Bake (around 103449), past the Horse Isolation Hospital (110438), through Fargo Plantation to Lake Down Aero- drome at Druid's Lodge, with spurs to the RAF/Handley-Page hangars at 110427 (Pl. 12) and to the Stonehenge Aerodrome at 11704185, the buildings of which lay on either side of the A303 and were subsequently known as Stonehenge Pedigree Stock Farm (Pl. I).

Most of the light railway appears on OS 6-inch 2nd ed. revised 1923, but air photographs show that dis- mantling of the line had begun a year or two earlier and that by about 1932 most of the rails had been lifted leaving only the track bed. Some of the latter still survives in the form of shallow cuttings and embankments. The railway appears to have caused relatively little damage to antiquities. It passed among but avoided the barrows at Winterbourne Stoke Cross Roads (Pl. 2); N of the Packway it exposed a burial at 114448 (p.7). Construction of one of the installations it served, the Balloon School at Rolle- stone Bake, appears to have been responsible for much damage to the group of round barrows Shrewton (14–21). The extensive hutted encampment (partly visible in Pl. 11) built during the First World War at the E end of the Stonehenge Cursus, and immediately adjoining its N side, no doubt contributed to the obliteration of its bank and ditch which in that sector is now quite untraceable.

INVENTORY OF MONUMENTS

BARROWS AND OTHER BURIAL SITES
(*see* Editorial Notes p.viii)

LONG BARROWS
Air photographs suggest the presence of two long barrows not certainly recorded hitherto.

AMESBURY
(140) Levelled barrow (14184194) on the E slope of a spur N of West Amesbury appears as crop-marks of parallel ditches about 20 m long and 12 m apart, aligned SSE-NNW. It lies on the N side of a group of round barrows/ring-ditches and a large ring-ditch (139) impinges on the SE end slightly E of the axis. This may be the site first recorded by Lukis (1864, 155): 'At West Amesbury was a long barrow (now destroyed) with a cist at one end.' Cunnington (1914, 408) assumed that the description indicated a chambered barrow and this interpretation is followed in VCH *Wilts* I (i), 137 (Amesbury 104). In the nineteenth century the term 'cist' was often applied to a simple pit or grave dug into the sub-soil; it is possible that, in the present instance, the 'cist' may have been the circular feature visible on air photographs (NMR SU 1441/17/18-21) at the centre of the ring-ditch.

WINTERBOURNE STOKE
(71) Levelled barrow (101409) lies on a gentle SE slope SSE of Longbarrow Cross Roads; appears as crop-marks of parallel ditches about 50 m long and 18 m apart, aligned NE-SW.
NMR SU 0941/7/86-8; 1040/1/30-1. OS 70 067: 144-5.

MONUMENTS FORMERLY CLASSIFIED AS LONG BARROWS
Two monuments hitherto classed as long barrows can no longer be accepted as such and are shown as round barrows on Maps 1 and 2. They are Amesbury 10a (VCH *Wilts*, I (i), 137; *OS Map of Neolithic Wessex*, no. 67) and Durrington 63-65 (VCH *Wilts*, I (i), 140, 172; *OS Map of Neolithic Wessex*, no. 79).

Amesbury (10a; 11944217), W of Stonehenge, described as a long barrow by Hoare (1810, 128), was excavated by him without result; it is shown on his map (Pl. 1) as a small elongated mound. It now appears as a low, ill-defined mound, about 18 m across, slightly elongated ENE-WSW. None of the numerous air photographs taken between the early 1920s and c.1970, while the site was still under cultivation, shows evidence for side-ditches, although the ditches of adjacent round barrows have often produced conspicious crop-marks.

Durrington (63-65; 15134317), S of Woodhenge, was thought by Hoare (1810, 170) to be a composite monument, comprising three round barrows set upon a long barrow; on his Map of the Amesbury Station it is depicted as a long barrow, but elsewhere (Pl. 1) he shows the alignment of three round ones. The site is still a prominent feature on the

ground, but former ploughing has obliterated details. Air photographs (NMR SU 1543/84 and 131; CUAP AR 55), taken when the N side was under cultivation, show what appear to be three circular mounds overlying a broad ridge of chalk, possibly accentuated by later disturbance; no ditches are visible.

LONG MORTUARY ENCLOSURE
WILSFORD CUM LAKE
Long mortuary enclosure (11424100), on Normanton Down, excavated by Mrs F. de M. Vatcher in 1959 (Vatcher 1961), aligned ESE-WNW, was 36 m in length overall and about 21 m wide, defined by discontinuous ditches and an internal bank. Remains of a structure, perhaps a portal, within the entrance at the ESE end, comprised a pair of short parallel bedding-trenches, each of which had contained three upright posts supported by horizontal timbers. No human remains were recovered. Finds included eleven antler picks, bones of ox and sheep or goat, and a sherd from the rim of a Peterborough bowl (Mortlake style) from a high level in the ditch. A radiocarbon date of 2560 bc ± 103 (BM-505) was obtained from an antler pick after publication of the report (CBA *Radiocarbon Index* 3C.3).

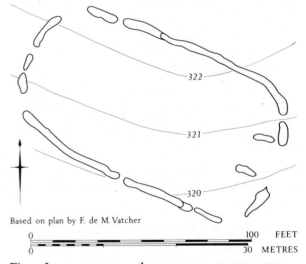

Based on plan by F. de M. Vatcher

```
0                              100   FEET
0                              30    METRES
```

Fig. 1. Long mortuary enclosure, NORMANTON DOWN

ROUND BARROWS
AMESBURY
(107-11) Five small barrows (11544180 to 11614181 approx.), no longer traceable, aligned along the N edge of the A303, immediately S of barrows (1) and (3), are described by Hoare (1810, 126) and shown on his map (Pl. 1).

(112) Ring-ditch (11144269), within s end of Fargo Plantation; ditch 0.3 m deep and 17.5 m in overall diameter encloses a flat area 12 m in diameter.

(113) Levelled barrow with outer bank (11384327), E of Fargo Plantation; soil-marks; RAF 106G/UK/915: 4205; CUAP ANG 29 and SE 54.

(114) Ring-ditch (11534276), immediately s of (49) in the Cursus Group; soil-mark about 6 m in diameter; NMR SU 1142/16/249-50.

(115) Bowl barrow (11764254), s of the Cursus Group; mound 0.1 m high, 12 m in diameter overall, with slight indications of ditch; ditch visible on RAF 106G/UK/915: 3205.

(116) Levelled barrow (13264303), s of the Cursus; soil-marks; RAF CPE/UK/1811: 4355.

(117) Levelled barrow (13074161), NE of Luxenborough Plantation; shown as 'Tumulus' on OS 2-inch map, 1808; soil-marks on RAF 540/854: 3458.

(118) Levelled barrow (13034152), NE of Luxenborough Plantation; soil-marks on OS 'Durnford' 5674 and on RAF 540/854: 3458; ring-ditch on NMR SU 1341/7/22-6.

(119) Ring-ditch with central dark spot (13534156), on Coneybury Hill; crop-mark; RAF 58/3250: 0007-8; CUAP NP 44.

W of the New and Old King Barrows

(120) Levelled barrow (13374208); soil-mark; NMR SU 1342/12 and 19.

(121) Levelled barrow (13364215); soil-mark; NMR SU 1342/12.

(122) Levelled barrow (13404220); soil-mark; NMR SU 1342/12 and 19.

(123) Levelled barrow (13354227); soil-marks; NMR SU 1342/19; SU 1242/76.

(124) Levelled barrow (13384254); soil-marks on NMR SU 1242/76; parch-mark on NMR SU 1342/23.

(125) Levelled barrow (13164263); soil-marks; NMR SU 1043/1/7-8; SU 1242/76 and SU 1342/37.

(126) Ring-ditch (13224270); soil- and crop-marks; OS 70 067: 210-1; NMR SU 1043/1/7-8; SU 1342/34; CUAP BI 49.

(127-8) Two contiguous levelled barrows (13354280, 13354281); soil-marks; RAF CPE/UK/1811: 4354-5.

(129) Ring-ditch (13694300); crop-mark; OS 70 067: 209-10; NMR SU 1043/1/7-8.

E of the New and Old King Barrows

(130) Levelled barrow (13584226); faint soil-mark; NMR SU 1342/45/254-6.

(131) Ring-ditch (13934226); soil-mark on OS 'Durnford' 5663, 5673; parch-mark on NMR SU 1342/57.

(132) Levelled barrow (13974226); see 'Barrow Excavations'.

(133) Levelled twin bell barrow (14004227); see 'Barrow Excavations'.

(134) Ring-ditch (13764292); crop-mark; OS 68 207: 374 and 70 067: 210-1.

(135) Levelled barrow (13834304); soil-mark; RAF 106G/UK/915: 4200-1; OS 70 067: 209-10.

N of West Amesbury

(136-8) Three aligned ring-ditches (14204182, 14224181,

14254180); crop-marks; NMR SU 1441/18/175. The SE member (138) is composite, with segmented inner ditch.

(139) Ring-ditch (14194192); crop-mark; NMR SU 1441/17/18-21. The ditch, with a circular feature at the centre, is set against the SSE end of the small long barrow (140), slightly to the E of the axis, and is interrupted at the point of intersection.

N W of Vespasian's Camp

(141) Levelled barrow (14304218); crop-mark; NMR SU 1342/28 and SU 1442/16.

(142) Ring-ditch enclosing a segmented inner ditch (14334225); crop-mark; NMR SU 1342/28; SU 1342/48/423-4; SU 1442/20/170-1.

(143) Ring-ditch (14424228); parch-mark; NMR SU 1342/28 and SU 1442/4.

N of Vespasian's Camp

(144) Levelled barrow (14484238); soil-marks on OS 'Durnford' 5663 and on NMR SU 1442/16; crop-mark on SU 1442/23/186-7.

(145) Levelled barrow (14454260); soil- and crop-marks on RAF 106G/UK/915: 3199-200 and on NMR SU 1442/18/95-7; two concentric ditches visible on NMR SU 1442/23/186-7.

(146) Levelled barrow (14594260); soil-mark on OS 'Durnford' 5672 and on RAF CPE/UK/1811: 4351-2; crop-mark on NMR SU 1442/23/186-7.

(147) Ring-ditch (14444275); crop-mark on OS 70 067: 154 and 209; NMR SU 1342/28.

(148) Ploughed-down barrow (14434279), shown in incorrect position on OS 6-inch map, 1961; crop-mark on RAF 58/3250: 0019: NMR SU 1342/28; OS 70 067: 154.

(149) Levelled pond(?) barrow (14424298 approx.); parch-mark on NMR SU 1442/28-9; crop-mark on SU 1442/24/188-9.

(150) Levelled barrow (14424303); soil-mark on RAF CPE/UK/1811: 4352-3; parch-mark on NMR SU 1532/1/028-9 and SU 1442/28; crop-mark on SU 1442/24/188-9.

(151) Levelled barrow (14854250); soil-marks; NMR SU 1442/1, 4 and 11.

S W of Totterdown Clump

(152) Ring-ditch (15094294); crop-mark on RAF 58/3250: 0019; parch-mark on NMR SU 1543/170.

(153) Ring-ditch with irregularly spaced pits or post-sockets on the perimeter (15154296); parch-marks; NMR SU 1543/170.

A further 10 possible round barrows for which the evidence is uncertain are noted below. These sites are not included in Maps 1 and 2.

Part of a narrow circular ditch (11324177), N of the A303; soil-mark; RAF CPE/UK/1811: 4357-8.

Circular mark (11894290), s of the Cursus; soil-mark on NMR SU 1043/1/5-6; semicircular crop-mark on SU 1143/2.

'Tumulus' (12874140), within Luxenborough Plantation, first appeared on 1926 edition of OS 6-inch map; marked as destroyed on 1:10,000 map; no other record.

Circular mark (13734182), SE of the New King Barrows; crop-mark on NMR SU 1442/16; faint soil-mark on SU 1442/4-5.

Dark soil-mark suggestive of a pond barrow partly obscured by a track (13754305), E of the Old King Barrows; RAF 106G/UK/915: 4200-1; NMR SU 1343/4.

Circular soil-mark (13884310), E of the Old King Barrows; RAF 106G/UK/915: 4200-1.

Two circular soil-marks (14234232, 14294232), NW of Vespasian's Camp; OS 'Durnford' 5663 and 5672-3; NMR SU 1342/28 and SU 1442/4.

Circular soil-mark (14544224), N of Vespasian's Camp; OS 'Durnford' 5663 and 5672; NMR SU 1442/9.

Circular soil-mark (14844293), NE of Vespasian's Camp; RAF CPE/UK/1811: 4352-3; NMR SU 1442/1.

DURRINGTON

(72) Levelled barrow (11344415), N of Fargo Road; OS 2-inch map, 1808; NMR SU 1144/2-3.

(73) Mound, probable barrow (13194323), N of the Cursus; chalky mound, 0.1 m high, 6 m in diameter; OS Records.

(74) Ring-ditch (14974324), SW of Woodhenge; soil-mark; OS 'Durnford' 5663, *see also* 'Barrow Excavations'.

(75) Levelled barrow (14734314), just N of parish boundary; soil-marks; RAF CPE/UK/1811: 4353.

Destroyed mound (11834400 approx.), S of barrows (20) and (21); recorded as 'not sepulchral' by Hoare (1810, 167, no. 80), but shown on his map (Pl. 1).

WILSFORD CUM LAKE
Within the Lake Wood Group
(45c) Not an additional barrow but one incorrectly placed in VCH *Wilts* I (i), 198. It is no. 13 in Hoare's illustration of the group (1810, opp. p.207) and must, therefore, be further E than 10974022. It survives, in fact, as a low mound 10 m across and 0.2 m high at 11024030.

(89) Bowl barrow (10774023), immediately E of barrow (37); *see* 'Barrow Excavations'.

(90) Ring-ditch (10784023), between barrows (89) and (38); *see* 'Barrow Excavations'.

(91) Levelled barrow(s) (10784022), immediately SSW of barrows (38) and (39); chalky soil-mark suggests two small confluent mounds or an 'oval' mound; NMR SU 1040/3/53-4. A contour survey (Grimes 1964, fig. 2) appears to indicate the N end of this feature.

(92) Bowl barrow (10874017), SE of barrow (40), appears to correspond with a barrow shown on Hoare's map (Pl. 1), but not numbered or mentioned in the text. The mound, 0.9 m high and 19.0 m in diameter, is enclosed by a shallow ditch.

(93) Ring-ditch (11304049), in the centre of the 'North Kite'; shadow-site on NMR SU 1140/4; crop-mark on RAF 540/854: 4329-30.

(94) Ring-ditch (12704053), NE of Springbottom Farm; crop-mark; RAF 540/854: 3159 and 4328.

(95, 96) Two ring-ditches (13124069, 13144072), NW of Springbottom Farm; soil-marks on OS 70 067: 140-1; OS 'Durnford' 5682; RAF 58/3250: 0008; crop-marks on NMR SU 1340/3/27-9, 1340/5/165-6, 1340/6/167.

(97) Levelled barrow (13214032), NW of Normanton; soil-mark; CUAP RC 8 BV 8-9.

(98) Levelled barrow (13524092), S of Coneybury Hill Plantation; faint soil-mark; RAF 540/854: 4326.

(99) Ring-ditch (13574058), S of Coneybury Hill Plantation; crop-mark; NMR SU 1340/1-2.

(100) Ring-ditch (12073870), WNW of Rox Hill Clump lies immediately W of a boundary ditch; crop-mark; NMR SU 1238/3; 1238/6.

(101) Ring-ditch with central dark spot (12263878), on the N side of Rox Hill; crop-mark; NMR SU 1238/2-3.

(102) Ring-ditch (12173857), SW of Rox Hill Clump; crop-mark; NMR SU 1238/4.

WINTERBOURNE STOKE
(72) Levelled barrow (09824177), SW of the Winterbourne Stoke Cross Roads Group; soil-mark on NMR SU 0941/2/26-9; segmented ditch shows as parch-mark on NMR SU 1041/8 and as crop-mark on SU 0941/7/86-8.

(73) Levelled barrow, possibly with outer bank (09904194), W of the Winterbourne Stoke Cross Roads Group; crop- and soil-marks; NMR SU 1041/32/65-6 and 1041/33/67-9.

(74) Ring-ditch (10024110), S of the Winterbourne Stoke Cross Roads Group; crop-mark; NMR SU 0939/5/209-10; SU 0941/7/86-8; OS 70 067: 145.

(75) Levelled barrow with outer bank (09704421), in alignment with barrows (45) and (70); soil-marks; NMR SU 0939/5/211 and SU 1049/8/167.

(76) Destroyed barrow (10434203 approx.), immediately NE of barrow (22); mentioned by Hoare (1810, 126) in conjunction with (22) and shown as a small mound on his map (Pl. 1); numbered [22a] by Goddard (1913, 364); omitted from VCH *Wilts* I (i).

(77) Levelled barrow with outer bank (10384200), immediately SW of barrow (22); soil-marks; NMR SU 1041/11/73-4. Thurnam (1870, 309, note c) mentions 'two or three very small mounds', from one of which, possibly (22), he recovered a Bucket urn (*ibid.*, 353, note c, pl. XXX:6).

(78) Ring-ditch (10124292), E of the A360; crop-mark; NMR SU 1043/1/3-4.

(79) Bowl barrow (10384238), between the A360 and the parish boundary; the mound, 0.3 m high and 19 m in diameter, is enclosed within a ditch. OS Records.

(80) Bowl barrow (10344224), between the A360 and the parish boundary; the mound, 0.3 m high, is 14 m in diameter. OS Records.

(81) Levelled barrow (10744261), SW of Fargo Plantation; soil-marks; OS 70 067: 148-9; RAF CPE/UK/1811: 4357.

(82) Levelled barrow (10734269), SW of Fargo Plantation; soil-marks; CUAP ANG 30-1; RAF CPE/UK/1811: 4356-7; NMR SU 1041/1/14 and 1043/1/5.

NE of Greenland Farm
(83) Levelled barrow (10104422); soil-marks; NMR SU 0939/5/211 and 1049/8/167; RAF 58/3250: 0022.

(84) Levelled barrow (10074430); soil-marks; NMR SU 0939/5/211 and 1049/8/167; RAF 58/3250: 0022.

(85) Barrow with outer bank (10064435); soil-marks on NMR SU 0939/5/211 and 1049/8/167; parch-mark of ditch on OS 73 300: 036. The mound is 0.2 m high; the bank and ditch, about 30 m in diameter overall, are just traceable on the ground.

Destroyed mound (09664306 approx.), SE of barrow (42), was described by Hoare (1810, 166) as a 'landmark' but included on his map (Pl. 1).

WOODFORD

(17) Levelled barrow (10153917), ENE of Druid's Lodge; soil-mark on OS 70 067 : 077; parch-mark on NMR SU 1038/1/39-40 and on SU 1039/2/74.

(18) Penannular ditch (10203915), ENE of Druid's Lodge; parch-mark about 50 m in diameter, with gap at SW; bisected by field boundary; NMR SU 1038/1/39-40.

BARROW EXCAVATIONS
(*see* Editorial Notes, p.viii)

AMESBURY

(39) Bowl barrow enclosed by a ditch (13154204), W of the New King Barrows, previously excavated by W. Cunnington (Hoare 1810, 159, no. 26), was re-excavated by Mr Paul Ashbee in 1960 (interim report in *PPS* xxvii (1961), 345). Mr Ashbee has kindly provided additional information in advance of publication of his definitive report. The burnt remains of a pyre or mortuary structure have yielded a radiocarbon date of 1670 bc ± 90 (HAR-1237); there were indications of burning *in situ* beneath the mound. Grave-goods recovered by Cunnington comprise beads of amber and shale and a V-bored shale button (Annable and Simpson 1964, 60, nos. 467-72). A few sherds, probably from a Globular urn, came from the upper fill of the ditch. Much occupation debris, including sherds of Earlier Neolithic, Peterborough and Grooved Ware, worked flints and animal bones, had been incorporated in the loam core of the mound. The barrow has been restored to its pre-1960 appearance.

(51) Bowl barrow (11434273), S of the Cursus, previously excavated by W. Cunnington (Hoare 1810, 163, no. 36), was re-excavated by Mr Paul Ashbee in 1960 (Ashbee 1978). The proposed sequence, which takes into account the results of Cunnington's excavation and apparent anomalies or ambiguities in the records thereof, is as follows: (1) large central grave, provided with a mortuary house made of jointed timbers which contained a contracted male skeleton, together with large trephination roundel from his skull, and probably a Wessex/Middle Rhine Beaker; covered with surplus chalk from grave; (2) construction of barrow, separated by a narrow berm from a ditch composed of five segments; (3) contracted burial accompanied by a Wessex/Middle Rhine Beaker deposited in a grave cut through silt into the bottom of the ditch; (4) insertion of three secondary burials in mound: (a), at base, contracted skeleton, probably accompanied by a late Beaker (Developed Southern British: funnel-neck western variant) and perhaps by a folded hide; (b) contracted skeleton accompanied by a late Beaker (Developed Southern British: cylinder-neck eastern variant), two carbonized wooden implements, a double-pointed bronze awl together with antler slip, a roe-deer antler with protective sheath, an antler spatula, and a large flint scraper; (c) a contracted skeleton. A radiocarbon date of 1788 bc ± 90 (BM-287) has been obtained from one of the wooden implements with burial (b). Fragments of bluestone (rhyolite) were recovered from the chalk fill of the central grave, from the turf core of the mound and from the upper silt of the ditch. The barrow has been restored to its pre-1960 appearance. The finds from both excavations are in the Devizes Museum.

Two ploughed-out barrows, E of the New King Barrows, not previously recorded, were excavated by Major H. F. W. L. Vatcher in 1959 (interim reports in *WAM* lvii (1960),

394).

(132) Probable bowl barrow (13974226) surrounded by a ditch 18 m in diameter. No traces of interments remained. An elongated pit, off-centre, produced sherds of Earlier Neolithic pottery.

(133) A twin bell barrow (14004227), with oval ditch measuring 30 m on the long diameter, yielded two urns, both inverted over cremations, each set about 4.5 m from the centre; a quantity of cloth was also recovered from one of the urns. A small pit, marking the centre of the barrow, was filled with earth and capped by chalk. It had been cut into a larger hollow, perhaps of natural origin, which contained a sherd of Peterborough ware and the remains of an antler. Sherds of Grooved Ware were recovered from beneath the buried surface.

DURRINGTON

(74) A pipe-trench which passed through the ditch of this previously unrecorded barrow (14974324), WSW of Wood-henge, exposed Middle Bronze Age pottery, animal bones and two worked flints. Amongst material salvaged were fragments of a Barrel urn and a Globular urn (Stone, Piggott and Booth 1954, 166). The ditch can be seen as a very small circular soil-mark on OS 'Durnford' 5663.

WILSFORD CUM LAKE

Two bowl barrows (1) and (33), W of Normanton Gorse, excavated by W. Cunnington in 1805 (Hoare 1810, 206), were re-excavated by Miss E. V. W. Field in 1960 (interim reports in *WAM* lviii (1961), 30-1, and *PPS* xxvii (1961), 346).

(1) Bowl barrow (Hoare's no. 166; 11124163), about 15 m in diameter and 0.38 m high; Cunnington had found a skeleton, a 'drinking cup' and antlers in the central grave. This grave proved to have contained at least two inhumations and a cremation; fragments of a Beaker were recovered from the original fill. Eight more inhumations, all in the N side of the barrow, represented seven infants (burials 4-10) and the crouched skeleton of a young adult (grave 11). Burial 4 was accompanied by 'a small vessel of urn type', burials 5, 7-9 by Beakers, burial 10 by a Beaker, bone ring and pierced boar's tusk. Beaker sherds and a piece of slate shaped like a flat bronze axe came from the fill of grave 11. The Beaker from the central grave is of European type (Clarke 1970, 504, no. 1155); the remainder are of Wessex/Middle Rhine type (*ibid.*, nos. 1156-61); most of them have been illustrated (*ibid.*, figs. 67, 138, 182-3, 219).

(33) Bowl barrow (Hoare's no. 168; 10814136), about 24 m in diameter, ploughed almost flat; the central grave contained only cremated bones, previously disturbed by Cunnington.

Seven barrows, part of the Lake Wood group, were excavated under the direction of Professor W. F. Grimes in 1959 (Grimes 1964). They comprise barrows (36f), (36g), (37-39), and two, previously unrecorded, which were discovered between (37) and (38). These two, designated (38a) and (38b) in the report, appear on Fig. 15 as (89) and (90). The four larger barrows (36f, 37-39) had been excavated by W. Cunnington (Hoare 1810, 209-10). The finds from both excavations are in Devizes Museum.

(36f) Bowl barrow (Hoare's no. 2; 10741024), ploughed almost flat, enclosed by a ditch with inner diameters of

8.0 m and 7.5 m. Previous finds comprised a cremation accompanied by an 'incense cup' lying 'just under the surface' (Hoare 1810, 209, pl. xxx:1). Re-excavation revealed a disturbed primary cremation in a central pit and two satellite inhumations placed on the E-W axis, each at the inner edge of the ditch; one was the crouched skeleton of a male, the other of a female in a contorted posture, accompanied by an infant. A hole in the SE quadrant contained cremated bones. Unassociated finds comprised fragments of an All-over Cord Beaker and of Peterborough pottery, together with a few worked flints.

(36g) Bowl barrow (10764022), ploughed almost flat, enclosed by a shallow ditch with an inner diameter of 6 m. A central disturbance contained a few pieces of cremated bone and sherds of a Barrel urn; parts of the same urn had been recovered from rabbit-scrapes in 1950.

(37) Bowl barrow (Hoare's no. 3, recorded as previously opened; 10754024), about 0.3 m high, enclosed by a ditch with inner diameter of 14 m. Partial excavation revealed a disturbed central cremation pit containing one of Cunnington's lead plaques, dated 1804. Unassociated finds comprised fragments of Beakers (All-over Cord and indeterminate), Peterborough ware, part of the rim of a Collared or Biconical urn (in topsoil), and worked flints.

(38) Bowl barrow (Hoare's no. 4, recorded as previously opened; 10784023), about 0.6 m high, enclosed by a ditch with inner diameter of 13.75 m. Excavation disclosed seven pits, some of them not explicitly sepulchral in function. Pit (1), circular in plan and centrally placed, was disturbed but had probably contained an inurned cremation. The nearby pit (2), also disturbed, was elongated in plan and may not have held an interment. Pits (3) to (6) were disposed in an arc on the E side of the barrow, close to the ditch. Pit (3), sealed by the chalk rubble of the mound, contained an upright Collared urn and the cremated bones of an infant. Pit (5), with an inverted Collared urn and cremated bones of a child, and pit (6), with a small barrel-shaped vessel but no bones, may have been inserted after construction of the barrow had begun. Pit (4) yielded only fine ash and charcoal. The seventh pit, cut into by the inner edge of the ditch, through both primary and secondary silting, contained the cremated remains of two adults. A further interment, represented by a spread of burnt bones in a disturbed area at the sw edge of the mound, may have been associated with sherds of Late Bronze Age or Early Iron Age date. Pottery of similar type, a double-spiral ring and a piece of wire, both of bronze, and animal bones, scattered in the sw quadrant of the mound and extending over the fill of the ditch, also appeared to indicate post-barrow activity. Unassociated finds of earlier date comprise a rim-sherd of Ebbsfleet ware, two sherds from an All-over Cord Beaker, animal bones and flint flakes.

(39) Bowl barrow (Hoare's no. 5; 10794022), 0.6 m high, enclosed by a penannular ditch with inner diameter of 13.7 m; the ditch terminals had been cut into the chalky fill of the ditch of barrow (38). Fragments of burnt bone in the disturbed fill of a central pit may represent the residue of the cremation accompanied by a necklace of shale beads found by Cunnington (Hoare 1810, 210). An irregular hollow antedating the barrow yielded fragments of unburnt human bone, possibly from a disturbed burial; a sherd from an All-over Cord Beaker came from the edge of the hollow. Other finds contemporary with, or earlier than, the barrow comprised fragments of Peterborough and Beaker ware, worked flints, including a barbed-and-tanged arrowhead and scrapers, and animal bones. A Biconical urn, found at a high level in the fill of the ditch, yielded no evidence of funerary function.

(89) Small bowl barrow (numbered 38a in the report; 10774023), set midway between (37) and (38), 0.3 m high, enclosed by a ditch with an inner diameter of 5.5 m. A central pit, disturbed, yielded no finds.

(90) Ring-ditch (numbered 38b in the report; 10774022), intersected the ditches of (39) and (89) and was later than both. A central pit contained an upright Collared urn but no human remains.

Four barrows on Wilsford Down, all previously excavated by W. Cunnington in 1805 (Hoare 1810, 211), were re-excavated by Mr E. Greenfield in 1958 (interim reports in WAM lvii (1959), 228-9). The following accounts include additional information kindly supplied by Mr Greenfield in advance of his definitive reports. The conjectural correlations offered in VCH Wilts I (i), 198, between individual barrows on Wilsford Down and those described in Hoare's text are amended to accord with the results of these excavations. Discrepancies may be noted between Hoare's numbering and that in Cunnington's MSS accounts (kept in the library of the Wiltshire Archaeological and Natural History Society at Devizes) and between the relative positions of the barrows as shown on Hoare's plan of the Lake Group, on his map (Pl. I), and on Maps 1 and 2. The finds from the 1958 excavation, together with those that survive from the 1805 excavations, are in Devizes Museum.

(51) Bowl barrow (Hoare's Lake 22; 11494047), 0.38 m high, 15 m in diameter, enclosed by an irregularly segmented ditch. The primary grave, lying N-S, had been disturbed by Cunnington; part of an adult skeleton remained at a high level in a corner of the fill; sherds of a cord-ornamented handled vessel and of a middle-stage (North British/Middle Rhineland) Beaker were also recovered. Hoare reports that the grave, opened before 1805, contained unburnt bones, the remains of two 'drinking cups' (now lost), and another (a necked Beaker with finger-pinched decoration: Hoare 1810, pl. xxvIII:8; Annable and Simpson 1964, 41, no. 107; Clarke 1970, 504, no. 1168 and fig. 794) overlying the skeleton of a child. A circular pit, cut through the primary chalk mound, contained an undisturbed cremation; sooty soil, calcined flints and patches of charcoal incorporated in the mound make-up overlying this pit suggest scraped-up pyre material. A large quantity of Neolithic pottery in fresh condition and a few worked flints had been incorporated in this deposit; other Neolithic sherds were recovered from the ditch. The pottery includes Earlier Neolithic rim-sherds, Peterborough ware (Ebbsfleet, Mortlake and Fengate styles) and Grooved Ware. Two examples are illustrated by Annable and Simpson (1964, 36, nos. 10 and 11).

(52) Bowl barrow without ditch (Hoare's Lake 24; 11474045), the mound was completely destroyed. A large grave, disturbed by Cunnington, retained the remains of three superimposed inhumations above a possible primary cremation (Burial 1) represented by a few scraps of burnt bone and charcoal-flecked chalky soil. Burial 2 was that of a child accompanied by a necked Beaker ornamented with stab-marks (Annable and Simpson 1964, 42, no. 123;

Clarke 1970, 504, no. 1172 and fig. 971). Burial 3, an adult almost destroyed by the insertion of Burial 4, was accompanied by a Wessex/Middle Rhine Beaker (Annable and Simpson 1964, 42, no. 124; Clarke 1970, 504, no. 1171 and fig. 159). Burial 4, another adult, had been partly scattered by Cunnington. Hoare records a cremation with 'fragments of a drinking cup (lost) immediately under the turf'; two feet lower was another cremation immediately over the head of a skeleton (Burial 4?) and beneath this a second skeleton (Burial 3?). Fragments of Earlier Neolithic pottery and of Grooved Ware were scattered through the filling of the grave; many Earlier Neolithic sherds and a few of Peterborough ware were recovered from the upper fills of a series of hollows of natural origin in the vicinity of the grave.

(53) Bowl barrow without ditch (Hoare's Lake 23; 11474042), 0.15 m high and 13.7 m in diameter. A few scraps of cremated bone remained in the conical hole described by Hoare.

(54) Bowl barrow (Hoare's Lake 21; 11554043), 0.3 m high and 10.6 m in diameter; a 'ditch', represented by a ring of shallow soil-filled hollows, was not centred upon the grave. The grave, which Hoare records as already disturbed by 1805, still retained part of the original fill in which were found part of a skull, with a battle-axe and a flat bronze dagger with three rivets (Annable and Simpson 1964, 43, nos. 143, 145). The battle-axe, made of preselite (Group XIII rock) from South Wales, belongs to Stage II in the typology proposed by Roe (1966, 238, no. 232). Earlier interments are implied by finds, nearly all unstratified, comprising fragments of three Beakers (All-over Cord, European, Wessex/Middle Rhine: Clarke 1970, 460, nos. 1173-5; Annable and Simpson 1964, 43, nos. 142, 144, 146) and six barbed-and-tangled arrowheads (*ibid.*, nos. 136-41). Pre-barrow occupation is attested by fragments of Earlier Neolithic and Peterborough wares.

(83) Bowl barrow with ditch (11583894), among the Lake Down Group, excavated by Col. J. P. Haslam in 1959 (interim report in *PPS* xxvi (1960), 344). A large grave contained a cremation. 'Bronze Age' sherds were recovered from the ditch.

WINTERBOURNE STOKE

(30) Bowl barrow (11014292), within the w end of the Cursus, previously excavated by W. Cunnington, who found an unaccompanied cremation (Hoare 1810, 165, no. 44), was re-excavated by Mrs P. M. Christie in 1959 (Christie 1963, 376-82). A narrow berm had separated the destroyed mound from a continuous ditch with an average diameter of 17 m. A central pit, undisturbed, contained a few cremated bones (adult). Two pairs of stake-holes, nearby, formed a trapezoid in plan. The crouched skeleton of a child, perhaps originally covered with flints, lay in the primary silt of the ditch. Pottery from the upper fill of the ditch includes fragments of a Collared urn, others probably from a Globular urn, as well as Iron Age and Romano-British sherds. Pre-barrow activity was attested by a hollow, partly removed by the ditch, which yielded pine charcoal and calcined flints.

Two barrows s of the w end of the Lesser Cursus, both previously excavated by W. Cunnington (Hoare 1810, 165), were re-excavated by Major H. F. W. L. Vatcher in 1961 (interim reports in *WAM* lviii (1962), 242).

(31) Bowl barrow with outer bank (Hoare's no. 47; 10314313), listed as an ordinary bowl barrow in VCH *Wilts*

1 (i), 202. The diameter overall was about 25 m. The mound, nearly levelled, covered an oval pit, perhaps that from which Hoare records a cremation; fragments of burnt bone remained in the disturbed fill.

(32) Bowl barrow (Hoare's no. 46; 10374311), about 19 m in diameter, enclosed by a continuous ditch. A Collared urn (described as 'rude' by Hoare) had been replaced in a circular pit; a stake-hole was found on either side of the pit. A second Collared urn, undisturbed, was recovered from a pit beneath the SE side of the mound.

(45) Bowl barrow (09894410), NW of the Lesser Cursus, excavated by Mrs P. M. Christie in 1964 (Christie 1970), proved to be a mound composed of scraped-up soil, 0.76 m high and 20 m in diameter; there was no ditch. A central pit, roughly rectangular in plan, contained the undisturbed but incomplete remains of two adult males, both cremated.

Six barrows situated to the w and the N of the Lesser Cursus, all but one previously excavated by W. Cunnington (Hoare 1810, 165, 166n), were re-excavated by the late Mrs F. de M. Vatcher in 1961 (interim reports in *WAM* lviii (1962), 241). Correlations between the letters employed to designate individual barrows in the reports and parish numbers were kindly provided by Mrs Vatcher.

(38) Bowl barrow (Hoare's no. 52; 10124344), 22 m in diameter, enclosed by a deep, narrow ditch. A pit contained an inurned cremation; stake-holes formed a rough rectangle round the pit; others appeared to represent part of an incomplete circle. The mound was composed of scorched earth ('the marks of intense fire' noted by Hoare), capped with chalk rubble.

(39) Bowl barrow (Hoare's no. 53; 10044342), 1.36 m high and 26 m in diameter, enclosed by a deep, narrow ditch. Hoare records 'a cist with ashes' near the centre. Four phases of activity were recorded: (1) construction of a trapezoidal mortuary house surrounded by a stake-circle 11.5 m in diameter; (2) mortuary house destroyed by fire; (3) a shallow grave containing a 'token' cremation in centre of mortuary house; (4) construction of a mound of turves capped with chalk rubble after decay of the stake-circle.

(46) Bowl barrow (Hoare's no. 57; 10394425), 17.5 m in diameter, enclosed by a ditch. Two unaccompanied cremations were found in 1961. Hoare's vague account refers to an interment accompanied by a bronze dagger (?), whetstone, bone 'tweezers' and other bone artefacts (all lost).

(47) Disc barrow (Hoare's no. 61; 10504430). The following sequence was recorded: (1) small stake structure constructed, subsequently burnt; (2) circular stake structure, 7.6 m in diameter, with passage, surrounding central grave containing a cremation, bronze knife and awl, beads of amber and jet, and part of a leather belt; (3) small, incomplete ring of stakes placed round top of infilled grave; area enclosed by outer stake structure, by then collapsing, filled with turf. A secondary cremation, on the berm of the barrow, was accompanied by a bronze awl; the grave, lined with basketwork, had been covered by a small mound. (An undecorated Collared urn is attributed to this barrow by Cunnington and Goddard (1896, 69, no. 261) and by Annable and Simpson (1964, 63, no. 503); the urn is not mentioned by Hoare (1810, 166)).

(49) Disc barrow (Hoare's no. 58; 10474435). An irregular stake-hole circle, 6.7 m in diameter, surrounded an empty grave.

(50) Disc barrow (Hoare's no. 59; 10544438). A stake-hole

circle, 7.3 m in diameter, surrounded a robbed grave which still contained a bronze awl.

FLAT GRAVES

AMESBURY

Grave within a small 'hengiform' enclosure (11254280) in Fargo Plantation, s of the Cursus (Fig. 2). The ditch, interrupted by two asymmetrical causeways aligned approximately N-S, surrounded a slightly sunken area 6.0 m by 4.0 m; there may have been an outer bank. The rectangular grave, its sides lined with turves and its top sealed with chalk rubble, contained an incomplete skeleton, apparently in articulation when deposited, accompanied by a late-stage Beaker (Developed Southern British: funnel-neck variant), and two cremations in shallow holes dug into the floor, one perhaps associated with a Ridged Food Vessel. A third cremation was subsequently inserted in the E corner of the grave; a fourth had been deposited in a hole close to the inner edge of the ditch. Small pits or post-holes had been dug near the N and S corners of the grave. A sherd from the rim of a Peterborough (Fengate style) vessel and a fragment of bluestone were recovered from the upper fill of the ditch (Stone 1938; finds in Salisbury Museum).

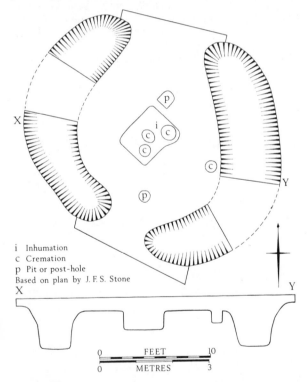

i Inhumation
c Cremation
p Pit or post-hole
Based on plan by J. F. S. Stone

0 ——— FEET ——— 10
0 ——— METRES ——— 3

Fig. 2. Flat grave, FARGO PLANTATION

Crouched inhumation (15204298), in the garden of 'Woodhenge', Totterdown, discovered in 1932 during tree-planting, lay with head to the S in a circular grave (Cunnington 1935). The position of the grave, in alignment with two ring-ditches (Amesbury 156 and 157, Map I), suggests that it may have lain within a ploughed-out barrow. Undecorated sherds, said to have been thrown out from the fill of the grave and now in Devizes Museum, are of Earlier Neolithic type.

Crouched inhumation in the ditch of Stonehenge, just w of the entrance, was discovered during excavations in 1978 (Atkinson and Evans, 1978). The skeleton of a young adult male lay in a grave cut into the ditch fill from the top of the secondary silting. It was accompanied by three barbed-and-tanged flint arrowheads and a stone wristguard.

DURRINGTON

Inhumation (148439 approx.), 'above Durrington Walls', in grave covered by a sarsen, accompanied by flint dagger, stone implement ('sponge-finger' stone), V-perforated button and pulley-ring, both of shale, and two small chalk discs (Hoare 1810, 172, pl. XIX; Annable and Simpson 1964, 39-40, nos. 86-90; finds in Devizes Museum).

Crouched inhumation (12264344), SW of Larkhill Camp, found c.1939 in oval grave, accompanied by two middle-stage Beakers, one undecorated, the other Wessex/Middle Rhine (Shortt 1946, 381-2; Clarke 1970, nos. 1108-9, figs. 188-9). Beakers in Salisbury Museum; National Grid reference is revised in accordance with the Museum's records. Grave erroneously attributed to Amesbury parish in VCH *Wilts* I (i), 28.

Contracted inhumation (12454393), W of Willoughby Road, Larkhill Camp, found in 1966 in narrow rectangular grave aligned N-S (Moore 1966). Skeleton in Salisbury Museum. National Grid reference has been revised by OS.

Crouched inhumation (114448 approx.), at Fargo, N of the Packway, found in 1918 during construction of a military railway (Stevens 1919). Skeleton in Salisbury Museum. Erroneously attributed to Amesbury parish in VCH *Wilts* I (i), 28.

Crouched inhumation found 'at Durrington' in 1916 during trench-digging, possibly at or near Larkhill Camp (1344) (*WAM* xli (1920), 184).

Inhumation burials were found in 1864 in an arable field near the boundary with Winterbourne Stoke (Ruddle 1901, 331) but it is no longer possible to locate them. About thirty were found but only two skeletons appear to have been in good condition, both laid N-S in shallow graves upon the chalk rock, here about a foot below the surface. In each case flints had been set 'like a low wall around the body and apparently above it.' The teeth of one of the skeletons were very worn. No grave goods are recorded.

Inhumation burial (14814365 approx.) was exposed in a trench dug through the bank of Durrington Walls in 1917 (Farrer 1918). The skeleton was said to be disarticulated and it is uncertain whether it had been inserted into the bank or was in the plough-soil overlying it. The skull and some of the bones were thought to show old fractures. It is not clear whether this should be regarded as an intrusive Beaker burial or one of much later date.

Two extended skeletons (14764366) were found in 1953 in a pipe-trench at a depth of about 0.6 m; they were unaccompanied (*Salisbury Journal*, 23.x.1953; Salisbury Museum records).

Inhumation cemetery (15144321), intrusive in barrow (67), was partly excavated by Mrs M. E. Cunnington (1929, 43-4; pl. 39). The remains of eleven adults lay in shallow graves cut into the NE side of the barrow; most were disturbed; one skeleton lay extended with the head to the south. Other graves were seen but left unexcavated because of lack of dating evidence. (These burials are not mentioned in VCH I (i), 172.)

CURSUSES, HENGES AND ALLIED SITES

AMESBURY

STONEHENGE

Much has been written on Stonehenge and here it is necessary to summarise only its building history. Professor R. J. C. Atkinson has contributed the following account of the structural sequence. The radiocarbon dates are corrected according to the scheme of R. M. Clark (1975). For a fuller discussion of the monument *see* Atkinson (1979). Photographs of Stonehenge appear as a central insert and on the front endpaper.

Period I

The surrounding ditch was excavated and the bank built within it, originally about 1.8 m high. Just within the bank the ring of 56 Aubrey Holes was dug and almost at once re-filled. Astride the axis of symmetry two stones were erected in the entrance of the earthwork, and a four-post structure some 20 m outside it. The adjacent Heel Stone belongs to this period; it may have been preceded by another stone, the hole for which was discovered in 1979 a few metres to the w of the Heel Stone, and cut by the surrounding ditch. The corrected date of an antler pick from the main ditch is 2810 BC ± 120 (I-2328, 2180 bc ± 105).

To the later part of this period belong the numerous cremations, some accompanied by Late Neolithic objects, inserted as secondary deposits in many of the Aubrey Holes

and in the bank and the silting of the ditch. The corrected date of a cremation from Aubrey Hole 32 is 2305 BC ± 280 (C-602, 1848 bc ± 275).

Period II

A new axis was adopted, directed approximately towards the summer solstice sunrise, and the entrance of the former earthwork was widened to fit it, by casting back part of some 8 m of the bank into the ditch on the SE side. From this reconstructed entrance the Avenue was built on the same axial alignment for a distance of about 530 m, to the nearer edge of Stonehenge Bottom, where a small low mound immediately to the SE appears to mark its termination. The corrected date for an antler pick from the bottom of the NW ditch of the Avenue, WNW of the Heel Stone, is 2135 BC ± 110 (BM-1164, 1728 bc ± 68). Another pick, from the bottom of the SE ditch about 30 m ENE of the Heel Stone and N of the A344, is dated 2190 BC ± 115 (HAR-2013, 1770 bc ± 100). The weighted mean of these two dates is 2160 BC ± 80.

The four Station Stones, two of them surrounded by a small ditch with an external bank, were probably erected at an early stage in this period, possibly even late in Period I. The finding of a large block of bluestone (preselite) in Bowls Barrow, an earthen long barrow 18.5 km WNW of Stonehenge, suggests that bluestones were already present in the

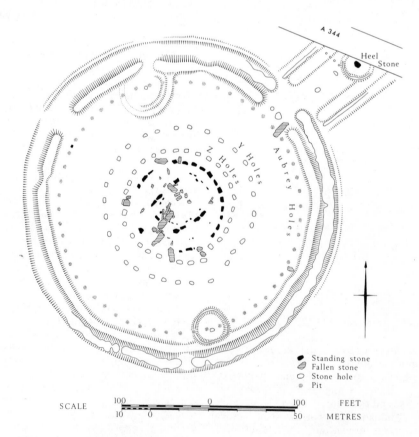

SCALE 100   0   100   FEET
10   0   50   METRES

Standing stone
Fallen stone
Stone hole
Pit

Fig. 3. STONEHENGE, general plan

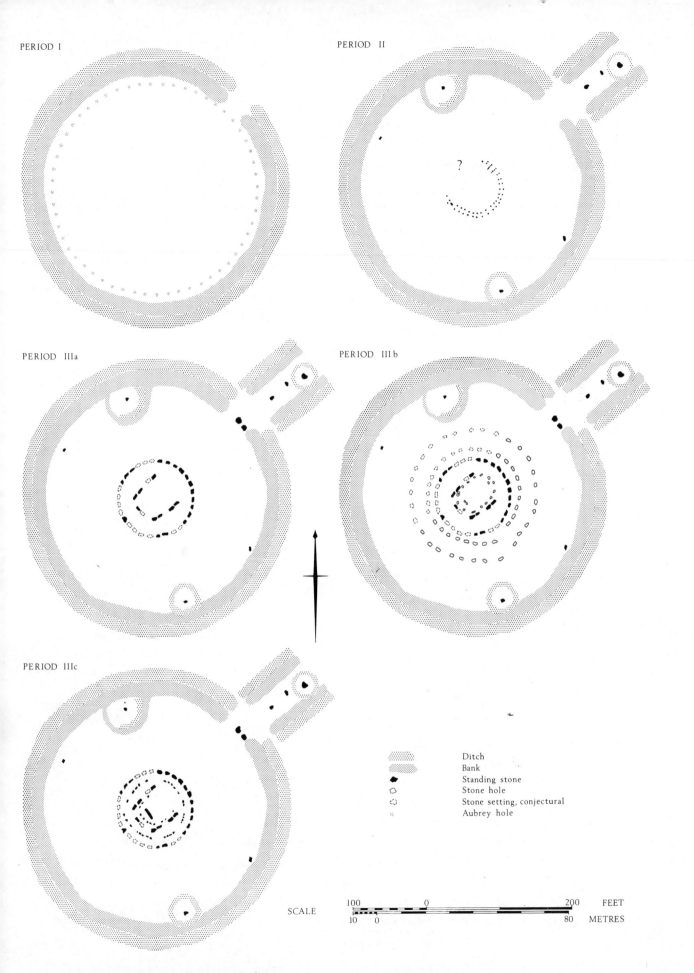

PERIOD I

PERIOD II

PERIOD IIIa

PERIOD IIIb

PERIOD IIIc

SCALE

100	0	200 FEET
10	0	80 METRES

Ditch
Bank
Standing stone
Stone hole
Stone setting, conjectural
Aubrey hole

Fig. 4. STONEHENGE, diagram of structural phases

area, although not at Stonehenge itself, during or even before Period I.

Probably at this stage the two stones in the entrance of Period I were re-set on the mid-line of the Avenue between the entrance and the Heel Stone. The latter was surrounded by a narrow ditch, almost immediately re-filled.

Concurrently or soon afterwards, the erection began of a double circle of bluestones in the centre of the monument, with an entrance marked by additional in-lying stones which was again aligned approximately on the solstitial sunrise. At the opposite end of the axial diameter there was a stone of exceptional size, perhaps the present Altar Stone. At least a quarter of this double circle, on the W side, was never completed. The stones already erected were dismantled, and the stone-holes re-filled. The corrected date of an antler pick discarded at this stage is 2000 BC ± 125 (I-2384, 1620 bc ± 110). If this date and the date for the erection of the largest

sarsen stone of Period IIIa below are taken as alternative estimates for the same event, the weighted mean date of the Stonehenge II/IIIa transition is 2045 BC ± 100.

Period IIIa

The large sarsen stones, originating on the Marlborough Downs, were erected in an outer ring of thirty uprights and an inner horseshoe of five trilithons, each capped by sarsen lintels. The preceding axis of symmetry was preserved, and a pair of close-set sarsen uprights, without a lintel, were placed astride the axis in the entrance of the earthwork, of which the Slaughter Stone survives. Station Stone 93 may have been replaced at this time. The corrected date for an antler pick sealed in the erection-ramp of the tallest sarsen stone (no. 56), which was probably the first to be raised, is 2120 BC ± 160 (BM-46, 1720 bc ± 150).

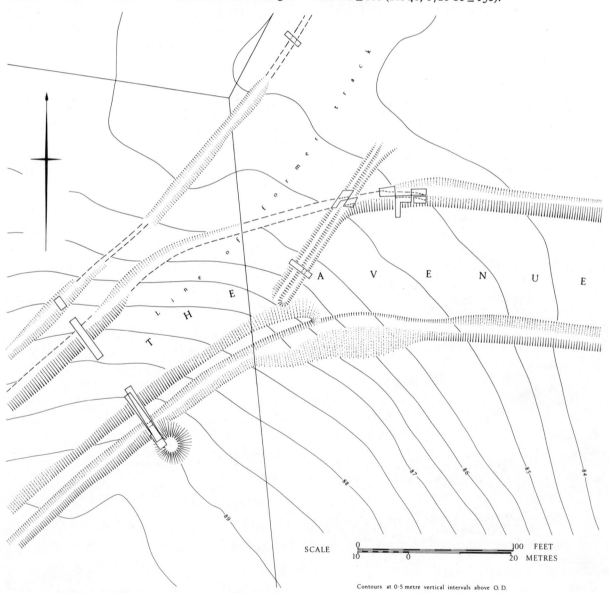

SCALE

Contours at 0·5 metre vertical intervals above O. D.

Fig. 5. STONEHENGE AVENUE, detail of the bend

Period IIIb

About twenty bluestones were selected and dressed to shape. These were erected in an oval structure which contained at least two miniature trilithons, following and closing the line of the later bluestone horseshoe. Later in the same period the two rings of Y and Z Holes were dug, probably with the intention of holding the remaining bluestones. This project was abandoned unfinished. The corrected date of an antler pick discarded on the bottom of Y Hole 30 is 1540 BC ± 120 (I-2445, 1240 bc ± 105).

Period IIIc

The re-arrangement of the bluestones in the present circle and horseshoe, with the Altar Stone (since fallen) standing on the axial line, presumably took place soon after the abandonment of the previous phase.

Period IV

The Avenue was extended eastwards from Stonehenge Bottom to the River Avon at West Amesbury. Animal bone and antler from both ditches where they are crossed by the Amesbury by-pass give a corrected date of 975 BC ± 115 (I-3216, 800 bc ± 100). Further specimens of antler from the NE ditch just N of West Amesbury House give a corrected date of 1345 BC ± 190 (BM-1079, 1070 bc ± 180). These two dates are not significantly different in the statistical sense. If they are treated as alternative estimates of the same event, the weighted mean date for the extension of the Avenue is 1075 BC ± 100.

The Avenue was built as the formal approach to Stonehenge and eventually linked it with the River Avon at West Amesbury some 2.5 km away. It consisted originally of twin parallel banks with ditches on the outside, but today less than one-third of the whole – the part nearest Stonehenge – survives in earthwork form; the remainder has been totally flattened by cultivation and is readily visible only from the air (Pls. 8 and 9; Map 1). From Stonehenge the Avenue extends downhill for some 530 m in a straight line towards the NE and then bends sharply ESE to cross Stonehenge Bottom. At the point where the bend begins a low mound abuts the S ditch and possibly served as a marking or sighting point for the construction of the straight initial section (Fig. 5). As well as being the best preserved this part of the Avenue is the most regular both in alignment and width; it measures 27.5 m across overall and the bank still stands 0.3 m above the bottom of the ditch (Fig. 6).

Beyond Stonehenge Bottom the Avenue, now levelled, continues in an almost straight line up the slop to the top of the ridge at Seven Barrows where, after passing between the Old and New King Barrows, it makes a broad curve and then continues SSE on a relatively straight alignment towards the river at about 142414. Air photographs show that throughout this section from Stonehenge Bottom eastwards

the ditches are less regularly spaced, especially E of the ridge (Pls. 8 and 9).

Rescue excavations have recently been carried out at three points along the course of the Avenue.

(i) Immediately N of Stonehenge, on the N side of the A344 (12334226), a section was cut by an electricity cable-trench (interim report in *WAM* lxiv (1969), 123). An antler pick and bluestone chips were recovered from the ditches. A radiocarbon date of 1770 bc ± 100 (HAR-2013) has subsequently been obtained from the antler pick, which lay on the bottom of the SE ditch. (A comparable date, 1728 bc ± 68 (BM-1164) is yielded by an antler pick recovered from the bottom of the NW ditch during Col. Hawley's excavations in 1923.)

(ii) On the course of the Amesbury by-pass (14004201) the ditches of the Avenue, here following an irregular course, were found to be 1.0 m to 1.95 m wide at the top and 0.4 m to 1.0 m deep (interim report in *WAM* lxiii (1968), 108). A radiocarbon date of 800 bc ± 100 (I-3216) has been obtained from animal bone and antler picks recovered from the bottoms of both ditches.

(iii) Immediately NW of West Amesbury House (14184153), where the Avenue approaches the River Avon (Smith 1973), only the ditch on the E side could be found. There were indications of the former presence of a bank on its W side. The ditch, which here passes through periglacial deposits (apparently a river terrace of Pleistocene age), was found to vary considerably in profile and in size in the course of some 36 m: from v-shaped to u-shaped, from 0.36 m to 1.80 m in width and from 0.15 m to 1.06 m in depth, according to relative hardness or softness of the subsoil through which it had been cut. There was no evidence of re-cutting; indications of deliberate back-filling, undated but probably pre-Roman, were observed in the deepest part of the ditch. Finds, comprising an indeterminate fragment of pottery, animal bones, pieces of antler and worked flints, were uninformative. A radiocarbon date of 1070 bc ± 180 (BM-1079) was obtained from antler after publication of the report.

These excavations indicate that the Avenue was built in at least two stages as described above; first the straight section from Stonehenge to the bend, and then the remainder. A late date for the E part of the Avenue finds some further support in its relationship to nearby round barrows, which might be expected to pre-date it if the above suggestion is correct. A distinct change or kink in its alignment, where it passes between round barrows Amesbury (100) and (131), suggests that the latter might well have been in existence when this part of the Avenue was built.

The Avenue, as noted above, has suffered much damage from subsequent human activity. Much of its eastern course lay within the unenclosed arable of West Amesbury and had already been flattened, and more was in process of being flattened, when Stukeley wrote his account of the monument

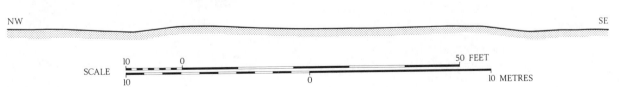

NW   SE

SCALE 10   0   50 FEET

        10   0   10 METRES

Fig. 6. STONEHENGE AVENUE, profile at SU 126425

Plate 8. STONEHENGE AVENUE and round barrows E of the King Barrows: looking s during drought of 1976

Plate 9. Remains of the STONEHENGE AVENUE, round barrows and ridge-and-furrow, E of the King Barrows, Amesbury: from the west. 1934

(1740, 35-7). From the top of the Seven Barrows ridge he noted that it 'still continues in the very same direction eastward, till unfortunately broke off by the plow'd ground, 300 feet from hence. This plow'd ground continues for a mile together, as far as the river's side at Ambresbury. So that 'tis impossible to trace it any farther. The first plow'd field, that southward, is Mr Hayward's; the other is of a different estate, call'd Countess Farm. And the plowing of these two go on at right angles one of another. That piece on the north side of the avenue, of the latter tenure, goes along the line of the avenue, is long and narrow, and has (as usual with greedy farmers) encroached upon and swallow'd up so much of the length of the avenue'. (Pl. 4). On the slope W of the Seven Barrows ridge the Avenue survived relatively undamaged into the early nineteenth century (Hoare 1810, 157-8) but by 1823 the upper part of the slope was in arable (WRO 283/202) and by the middle of the century the remainder appears to have been ploughed (Long 1876, 236).

In Stonehenge Bottom, however, the Avenue was already, in Stukeley's day, 'much obscur'd by the wheels of carriages going over it, for a great way together' on the road from Amesbury to Market Lavington (Pl. 5). Close by another track or road leading SW from Durrington breached the Avenue at the bend and followed it towards Stonehenge (OS 1-inch 1st ed. surveyed 1807-11). It is traceable today as a hollow way within the NW bank of the Avenue. This track would appear to have been in existence by the early eighteenth century and its course immediately N of the bend in the Avenue, emphasised for a short distance on the W side by what is now known to be a Bronze Age bank and ditch (Fig. 5; Map 1), led Stukeley (1740, 35 and Tab. XXVIII) to the mistaken conclusion that the Avenue bifurcated at the

bend and that one branch of it continued N towards the Cursus. This interpretation was accepted and perpetuated by Hoare (1810, 157-8).

A short length of bank and ditch blocks the Avenue obliquely and crosses its N side at the bend (Fig. 5); its sharper form, and the evidence of test excavations, show that it is of relatively recent construction, perhaps later than Hoare's time since it is not mentioned by him. Nearer to Stonehenge the Avenue is cut by the earthworks of an unfinished road (p.31). NMR SU 1242 and 1342 *passim*; 1441/17/18-21; 1441/18/174-5.

Henge monument on Coneybury Hill (13424160), totally flattened by ploughing, lies on almost level ground above 115 m OD and within sight of Stonehenge. The site was noted from the air in the 1920s and thought to be a disc barrow but later photographs (CUAP NP 44-7, QF 90, 92) show it to be a Class I henge with an entrance on the NE (King 1970). In plan the ditch is oval rather than circular, about 45 m by 55 m in overall diameter, with the entrance on the longer axis. Traces of an external bank are visible on an air photograph of 1934 (OS 'Durnford' 5674). The site appears never to have been recorded as a standing earthwork; probably it was levelled in medieval times or soon after. It lies within one of the former open-fields of West Amesbury, the Middle Field, a name first recorded in 1562 (Pugh 1947, 51). Traces of ridge-and-furrow impinging on the monument are visible on some air photographs (NMR SU 1341/4/156-8).

AMESBURY/WINTERBOURNE STOKE

Stonehenge Cursus (10954290-13704320) extends for nearly 3 km across undulating chalk downland some 700 m N of Stonehenge. It reaches a maximum height (110 m OD) at the ends which are intervisible and both within view of Stonehenge. From the W end, which lies on level ground, the Cursus extends down a shallow combe along a gentle N-facing slope where for part of its length it is out of sight of Stonehenge; it crosses the main dry valley known as Stonehenge Bottom and from there rises steadily to its E termination some 40 m short of the long barrow Amesbury (42) (Pl. 11). The Cursus varies in width overall from 100 m to 150 m and much of the enclosing bank and ditch survives,

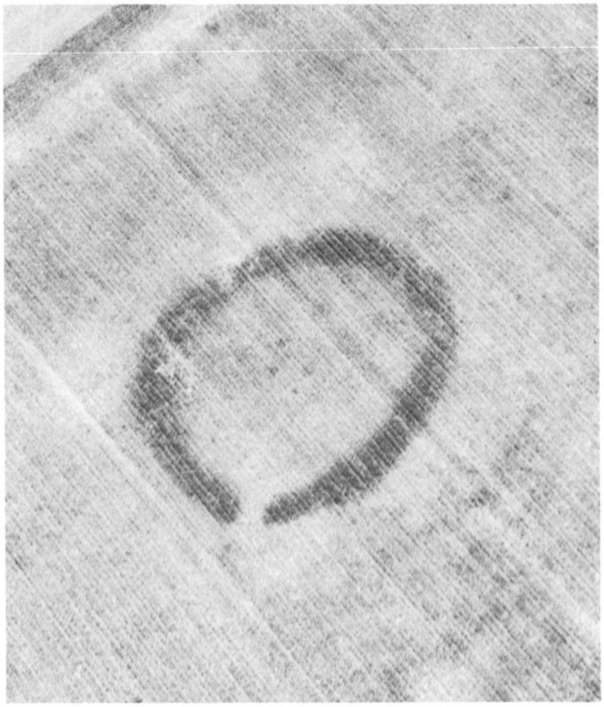

Plate 10. Henge Monument on CONEYBURY HILL, Amesbury, from the northeast. 1954

Plate 11. STONEHENGE CURSUS, the E end with long barrow. 1922

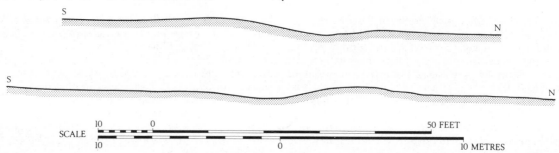

SCALE
10   0   50 FEET
10   0   10 METRES

Fig. 7. STONEHENGE CURSUS, profiles E of Fargo Plantation

particularly well preserved for some 1100 m E of Fargo Plantation. Further E still it has for the most part been damaged or levelled, and w of the Plantation it has been totally flattened. At best the bank is some 6.5 m across and 0.4 m high, the ditch of comparable width and depth. The ends are squarish in plan with rounded corners (Fig. 8, Pl. 12). Within Fargo Plantation a low bank (0.2 m high) with a ditch on the w side, measuring 6 m across overall, crosses the interior of the Cursus obliquely; its condition and

Stukeley (1740, 41) recorded opposed gaps in the Cursus towards the E end 'opposite to the straight part of Stonehenge avenue'. Hoare (1810, 158), following Stukeley, describes their position more precisely, i.e. 638 yards (583 m) w of the long barrow Amesbury (42) which he considered to be the E end of the Cursus. There are, however, grounds for doubting whether these gaps are truly original features. Air photographs (NMR SU 1343/1-2) taken in 1921-2, when the area was in cultivation, clearly indicate that the s bank and ditch were continuous at this point, and apparently the N bank also (the N ditch was not in arable), suggesting that any gaps were secondary.

A small excavation was carried out in 1947 on the s side of the Cursus 70 m E of Fargo Plantation (Stone 1947). At that point the ditch was steep-sided with a flat, even base, 1.8 m wide at the top and up to 0.75 m deep. A berm separated it from the bank which was 4.6 m wide and only 0.4 m high. In 1959 sections were cut w of Fargo Plantation (Christie 1963), and those on the N and s sides resembled in size and profile the earlier cutting, though slightly deeper (Fig. 8). At the w end, however, the Cursus was found to have a larger ditch, up to 2.75 m wide and 2 m deep, with a wider berm (2.5 m) separating it from the internal bank, and, in addition, an external bank.

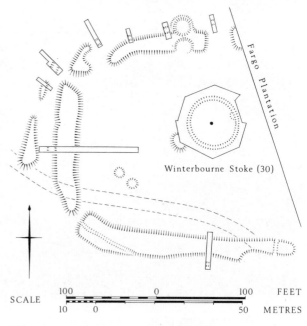

Winterbourne Stoke (30)

Fargo Plantation

SCALE
100   0   100   FEET
10   0   50   METRES

Fig. 8. STONEHENGE CURSUS, w end

Plate 12. STONEHENGE CURSUS, the w end to the N of buildings, probably early 1920s.

position suggest that it is contemporary with some phase of use of the monument rather than appreciably later, but on the s side its ditch appears to cut into the bank of the Cursus. West of the cross-bank and within the Cursus are two round barrows, Amesbury (56) and Winterbourne Stoke (30) (see 'Barrow Excavations', p.6).

PLATE I

Plate I. STONEHENGE and its immediate environs in 1928

PLATE II

Plate II. STONEHENGE, vertical air photograph, 1904

PLATE III

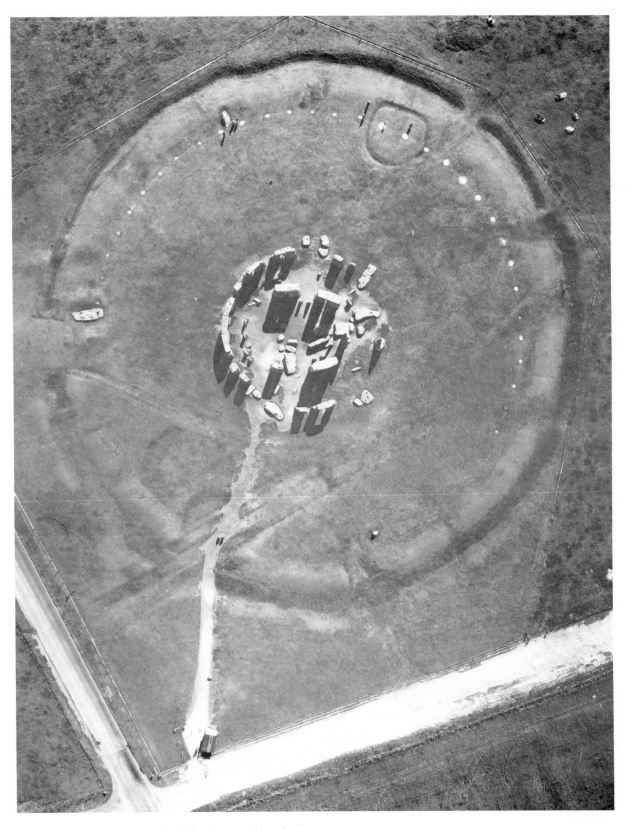

Plate III. STONEHENGE, vertical air photograph, 1962

PLATE IV

Plate IV. STONEHENGE from the SE in 1973

Stukeley (1740, 41-3) was the first antiquary to record, and possibly to recognise, the true nature of the Cursus. At that time it was apparently undamaged by ploughing and it appears to have remained so at least until the early nineteenth century when described by Hoare (1810, 159). The latter noted substantial damage from wheeled traffic on the road which crossed the monument in Stonehenge Bottom. By 1823, however, the part now within Fargo Plantation was in arable as were 300 m at the E end (WRO 283/202), and by 1879 (OS 6-inch 1st ed.) the latter had increased to 800 m. Further cultivation took place within and adjoining the Cursus and is visible on air photographs of 1921-2 (NMR SU 1143/2-5; 1243/1). The W end suffered damage when buildings for military purposes were erected almost on top of it during the First World War and subsequently used as a piggery; they have now been demolished. In Stonehenge Bottom construction of the outflow of the Larkhill sewage plant has further damaged the monument.

DURRINGTON

Durrington Walls (150437) is a large ceremonial monument or henge roughly circular in plan, 490 m by 468 m overall, with opposed entrances to NW and SE. It lies on a SE slope around a dry gully leading to the River Avon; the SE entrance faces the river some 60 m away. The earthwork had been 'for many years in tillage, its form much mutilated' when Hoare (1810, 169) recorded it, and the Tithe Map (1839) shows that it lay 'In Durrington Field', part of the former unenclosed arable of that village. As a result it is reduced in height and substantially modified in plan, to such an extent that the true nature of the earthwork has been revealed only relatively recently by air photography, geophysical survey and excavation.

The bank has survived as a spread feature on the E side some 40 m across, 2.5 m in height above the ditch and 1 m above the surrounding surface. On the N and W cultivation has reduced it to an inward-facing scarp which on the W side rises to a maximum of 5.5 m above the interior. The scarp continues along the S side but here it is a lynchet which, in part, has followed the line of the ditch; here the bank has been completely flattened. The ditch pursues a more irregular course than the bank and is separated from it by a berm which varies in width from 6 m on the NE and SW to 42 m on the SE. Air photographs suggest that the NW entrance is 29 m wide, the SE 22 m.

Excavations in advance of roadworks were made during 1966-7 along a N-S strip across the E side of the monument (Wainwright and Longworth 1971). The ditch was massive, 5.5 m deep, up to 17.6 m wide at the top and 6.7 m at the flat bottom. The bank was found to have been about 30 m wide. Within the enclosure the remains of two circular timber structures, akin to that at Woodhenge, were discovered on the line of the road but not central to it and, therefore, neither was totally excavated. The larger or 'Southern Circle' lay immediately within the SE entrance and comprised two main phases. The first was represented by four concentric rings of post-settings between 2.3 m and 30 m in diameter, with an entrance and a line of closely set posts, apparently forming a facade, on the SE. The second phase comprised a larger structure of six nearly concentric rings of post-holes between 5.6 m and 38.5 m in diameter; the outermost ring, possibly a slighter later addition, included two extra large post-holes presumably flanking an entrance, again on the SE side. Large quantities of pottery, flint and animal bones were found in an area of burning on a platform of chalk blocks and flint gravel outside the entrance and also in a midden which occupied a large hollow about 12 m long on the NE edge of the Circle.

The second or 'Northern Circle' also appears to have comprised two phases, but of the earlier little survived. The later structure consisted of a central arrangement of four large ramped post-holes set 5 m apart in a square, surrounded by a ring of smaller post-holes about 14.5 m in diameter. It was approached from the S by an avenue of two parallel rows of post-holes which was crossed by a surving line of close-set post-holes roughly concentric to the main circle and apparently forming a facade to it.

Grooved Ware was found in primary contexts at Durrington Walls in relation to the bank and ditch and also to the timber circles. Beaker pottery came from secondary silts in the ditch and from various contexts in the interior, none certainly primary. A series of radiocarbon dates for the monument was obtained as follows: from the base of the main enclosure ditch 1977 bc ± 90, 2015 bc ± 90,

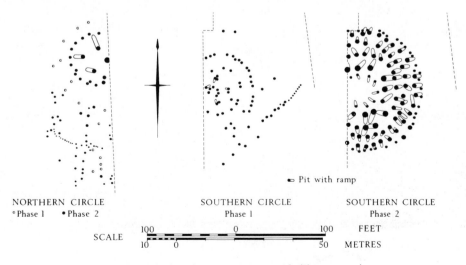

⊷ Pit with ramp

NORTHERN CIRCLE
○Phase 1   •Phase 2

SOUTHERN CIRCLE
Phase 1

SOUTHERN CIRCLE
Phase 2

SCALE

100   0   100   FEET

10   0   50   METRES

Fig. 9. DURRINGTON WALLS, interior structures revealed by excavation

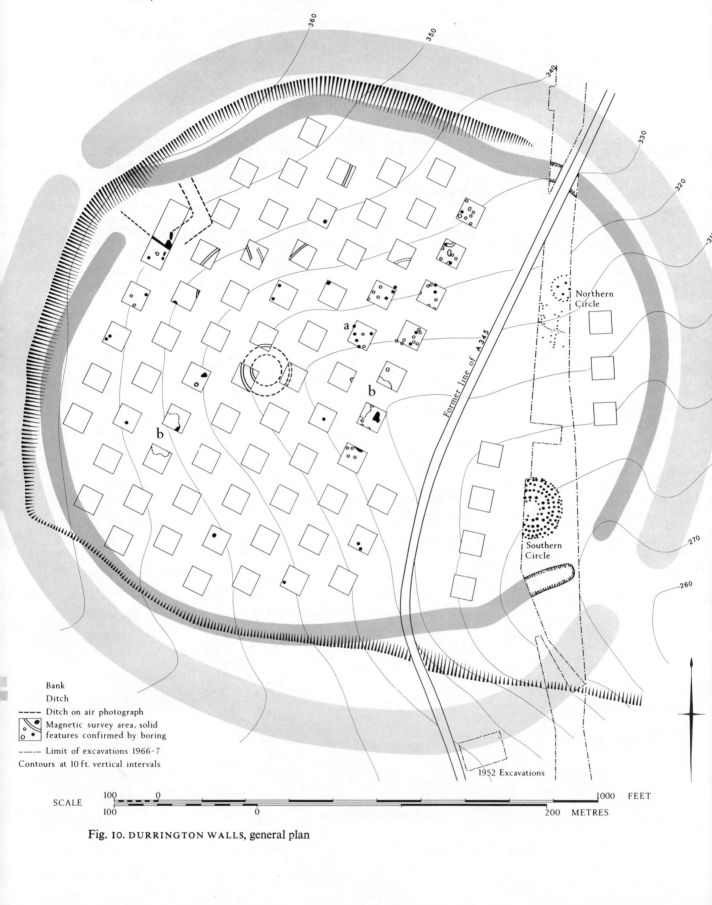

360

350

340

330

320

310

Northern
Circle

Former line of A 345

a

b

b

Southern
Circle

270

260

Bank
Ditch
---- Ditch on air photograph
Magnetic survey area, solid
features confirmed by boring
-·-·- Limit of excavations 1966-7
Contours at 10 ft. vertical intervals

1952 Excavations

SCALE

100   0   1000 FEET
100   0   200 METRES

Fig. 10. DURRINGTON WALLS, general plan

2050 bc ± 90 (BM-398-400); from the midden 2320 bc ± 95 (NPL-192); from the s Circle phase 1 1810 bc ± 148 (NPL-239); from the s Circle phase 2 1950 bc, 2000 bc, 1900 bc, all ± 90 (BM-395-7); and from the N Circle 1955 bc ± 110 (NPL-240). Hearths low down in the secondary filling of the ditch yielded dates of 1610 bc ± 120 and 1680 bc ± 110 (BM-285-6).

Remains of an earlier Neolithic settlement, including pottery, worked flints and bone, were found beneath the bank of the henge on the s side and yielded radiocarbon dates of 2634 bc ± 80, 2625 bc ± 50 (GRO-901, 901a) and 2450 bc ± 150 (NPL-191).

Beyond the area of the excavation relatively little is known of the interior of Durrington Walls. Air photography (Pl. 13) has indicated the presence of a small angular enclosure, about 45 m by 35 m, with gaps in its sides set immediately within the ditch and partly overlapping the NW entrance; and also of two concentric ditches, about 37 m across overall, just W of the centre of the monument (Crawford 1929). Recent geophysical survey of the interior on a sampling basis was carried out by Mr A. J. Clark (Anc. Mon. Lab.) who kindly contributed the following: The complete circuit of the ditch of the monument was traced, and the entrances confirmed, using electrical

resistivity supplemented by magnetic measurements, auger borings, and information from the aerial photographs published by Crawford (1929). Then, as part of the resurvey for the 1967 excavation, the site was marked out in 50 ft (15.2 m) squares and a sample of these surveyed by proton magnetometer at a spacing of 5 ft (1.5 m) between readings. Despite much magnetic interference from the rubbish that he saw being dumped, it was possible to define part of the sub-rectangular enclosure noted by Crawford at the western entrance, as well as the double ring-feature at the centre of the monument. Several minor ditches were detected, especially in the vicinity of the rectangular enclosure, suggesting that this was a later farm perhaps associated with the Romano-British remains excavated nearby. A scatter of other magnetic anomalies were interpreted as pits or large post-holes. Any patterns that may have existed in these are probably mostly lost in the coarseness of the survey, but are hinted at, for example, by the arc of four equally-spaced holes confirmed by boring at *a*. The broken outlines at *b, b* partially define areas where high readings indicate hollows that appear to contain occupation deposits. The soil is generally more than 1 m deep in the re-entrant at the centre of the monument. Archaeological features here must be better preserved than those on the chalk slopes on either

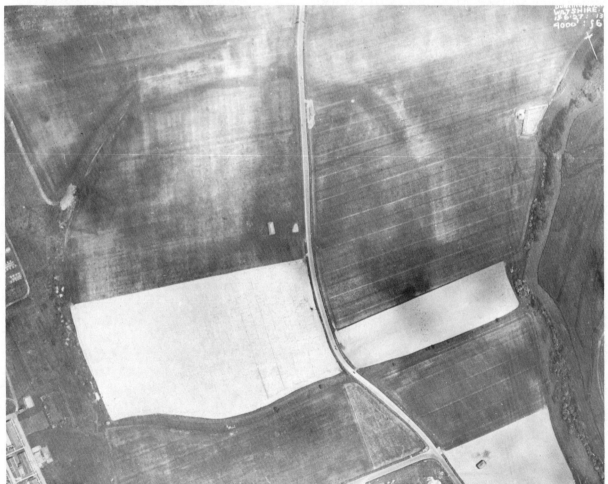

Plate 13. DURRINGTON WALLS, the Henge Monument in 1927, N to top

side, where the soil can be as little as 15 cm deep and where, as a result, plough erosion will have swept away most occupation levels and truncated the features that remain. No magnetic anomalies clearly of archaeological origin were evident in the two lines of squares surveyed on the E side of the old road.

A closer and more thorough magnetic survey with modern equipment would improve the definition of the features found, and would almost certainly reveal others.

Woodhenge (151434) lies immediately s of Durrington Walls at 100 m OD on a gentle E slope some 200 m from the River Avon and separated from it by a steep river-cliff. It had been almost totally flattened by ploughing and was thought to be a disc barrow until air photography in 1925 showed it to contain concentric rings of holes (Pl. 14). Excavations during 1926-8 (Cunnington 1929) revealed it to be a small henge monument circular in plan and measuring some 85 m across overall with a single entrance on the NE. It is now in the care of the Department of the Environment.

The ditch was found to be broad and flat-bottomed, up to 6 m across and 2.4 m deep; it was separated from the encircling bank by a narrow berm. Within the area enclosed by the ditch are six roughly concentric settings of post-holes arranged in an oval (marked today with concrete stumps), the outermost ring measuring 43 m by 40 m. The post-holes increase in depth and diameter from the outermost to the third ring; they are narrowest in the inner three rings but still deep. The larger holes had sloping ramps cut into them to facilitate the erection of wooden posts. It is reasonable to assume that all the post-holes are contemporary, there being no evidence to the contrary, and that they probably repre-

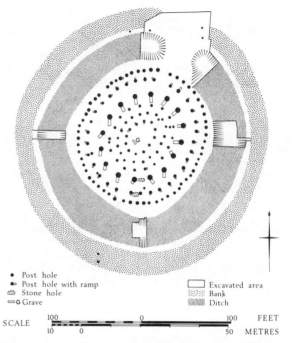

- • Post hole
- •◗ Post hole with ramp
- ◌ Stone hole
- ⌐G Grave

- ☐ Excavated area
- ▒ Bank
- ▓ Ditch

SCALE

100 ... 0 ... 100 ... FEET
10 ... 0 ... 50 ... METRES

Fig. 11. WOODHENGE, general plan showing excavated features

sent a timber building, whatever its precise form, rather than an arrangement of free-standing posts. A sarsen monolith (destroyed) may have been a later insertion between two posts of the second ring from the outside, at the south. A

Plate 14. WOODHENGE, round barrows and Bronze Age enclosure ('Egg') from the south. 1926

grave containing an infant burial, with the skull cleft in two, was found within the innermost ring of posts and a cremation in one of the post-holes (C14) of the third ring from the outside. On the E side of the monument a crouched inhumation was found in a grave cut into the bottom of the ditch before silting had begun. Fragmentary human remains, chiefly portions of skulls, were also recovered from primary and secondary positions in the ditch silts. Two infant inhumations, found high in the ditch, were associated with sherds of Romano-British pottery.

Earlier Neolithic pottery as well as Grooved Ware, other occupation debris and six pits, were sealed beneath the bank. Beaker pottery was found in secondary positions in the ditch and in the interior. Material recovered in 1970 (Burleigh *et al.* 1972, 397) from or near the bottom of a hitherto unexcavated portion of the ditch yielded radiocarbon dates of 1867 bc ± 74 (BM-677) and 1805 bc ± 54 (BM-678).

Woodhenge was apparently unknown to Stukeley and had probably been substantially flattened by cultivation before the eighteenth century. Hoare (1810, 170) described it as the 'mutilated remains of an enormous Druid barrow' (i.e. disc barrow). In 1839 (Durrington Tithe Map) it lay within an extensive area by then inclosed described as 'In Durrington Field', presumably a reference to a former openfield.

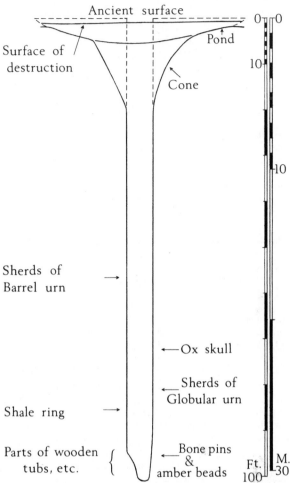

Based on schematic section by P. Ashbee

Fig. 12. WILSFORD SHAFT, section

Plate 15. The LESSER CURSUS, Winterbourne Stoke, from the west. 1951

WILSFORD CUM LAKE

Shaft (10864147). Excavation of a supposed pond barrow (Wilsford 33a), W of Normanton Gorse, revealed a cylindrical shaft 2 m in diameter and some 30 m deep (Fig. 0). Water-logged deposits at the bottom contained fragments of wooden vessels, pieces of rope and much other organic material. Wood from the bottom has yielded a radiocarbon date of 1380 bc ± 90 (NPL-74). Other finds from deep in the fill comprised sherds of Barrel and Globular urns, amber beads and bone pins. An Iron Age pot and Romano-British sherds were recovered from the fill of the weathering cone at the top (interim reports: *WAM* lviii (1961-3), 241, 468; Ashbee 1963).

WINTERBOURNE STOKE

The Lesser Cursus (10354345-10734352) lies immediately W of the N end of Fargo Plantation along the summit of a broad, flat-topped ridge. Air photographs show that it was still an earthwork in 1934 (os 'Durnford' 5667) but that by 1954 it had been effectively levelled by ploughing (RAF 106G/UK/915: 4206). Aligned WSW-ENE it is 400 m long and about 60 m wide overall and formerly comprised a bank with an external ditch of which only the latter survives. The

E end was never closed by a ditch, as air photographs confirm, and may have been unfinished. A bank and ditch crosses the cursus 200 m from the w end not quite at right angles to its main axis; it is accompanied by a constriction of the N and s sides. The position of the ditch on the w side of the cross-bank casts doubt on the obvious idea that the monument was built in two stages, the first a short cursus extending as far E as the cross-bank, the second an unfinished extension eastwards of it (Pl. 15).

NMR SU 1044/1; CUAP GF 46-8, LS 32-3.

SETTLEMENTS AND ENCLOSURES

AMESBURY

Four pits (15174313), in the garden of 'Woodlands', Countess Road, some 265 m SSE of the centre of Woodhenge (Stone and Young 1948; Stone 1949) were oval in plan, with maximum diameters ranging from 1.45 m to 0.91 m; their depths in the chalk subsoil varied from 0.76 m to 0.23 m. They contained: sherds of Grooved Ware, part of a stone axe made of Graig Lwyd rock (Group VII) from N. Wales, a flaked flint axe, other flint artefacts including transverse arrowheads and scrapers, bone points, antler picks, bones of domestic ox, sheep, pig and dog, remains of fox, frog, and a freshwater fish (chub), marine shells (scallop, mussel and oyster), carbonized nut-shells, pieces of sarsen stone including one with a smoothed surface, hammerstones and balls of flint, a few calcined flints and much charcoal and wood-ash. Two of the pits had been capped with flint nodules. The finds are in Salisbury Museum. (These pits are attributed to Durrington parish in VCH *Wilts* I (i), 65.)

Small pit (13224203), about 980 m ESE of the centre of Stonehenge, exposed by road-widening in the N verge of the A303, contained sherds of Grooved Ware, two chalk plaques bearing incised geometric motifs, animal bones and an antler pick (Vatcher 1969). (The National Grid reference is revised to accord with the position given in the report.)

Vespasian's Camp (146417), a univallate Iron Age hill-fort enclosing 15 ha (37 acres), occupies a strongly defensive position at the s end of a narrow spur partly within a meander of the River Avon. The domed interior of the fort rises to over 91 m OD; on the s the defences drop to below 69 m OD immediately overlooking the river.

The main rampart is a substantial bank along most of the w side, on the N and on the SE; elsewhere it was constructed, or survives, as a scarp with no surmounting bank. On the w, where it is best preserved, the bank stands up to 6.5 m above the ditch bottom and 2 m above the interior. Outside the ditch is a low counterscarp bank the outer face of which has been accentuated by the development of a negative lynchet beneath it. A broad shallow depression which runs immediately behind the main bank presumably provided additional material for its construction.

Along the s half of the E side, where the natural slope to the river is very steep, the defences have been modified by landscaping in the eighteenth century. A grotto, Gay's Cave, was built into the face of the rampart and ornamental paths constructed round it, all now heavily overgrown. South of Stonehenge Road the defences are generally less well preserved and have been damaged near the SW corner by tracks and quarrying. The main ditch survives only on the s side, as a narrow terrace along the face of the steep slope to the river. An undated hollow way leads from the sharp bend in the present road to West Amesbury past the SW corner of the fort to an apparent crossing of the Avon at the point where the main stream is divided by a small island.

An original entrance, somewhat widened, exists at the N end of the fort and before the construction of the by-pass could be approached along almost level ground from that direction. A further entrance is to be expected in a fort of this size and the sharp incurve of the rampart on the SE suggests that it may have stood at or just N of the point where Stonehenge Road passes through the defences.

During road-widening in 1964 the main rampart on the w side just N of Stonehenge Road was cut back revealing two phases of construction. An initial bank, of clean chalk and soil, stood 3 m above the original surface although its crest had gone. A dark soil horizon about 0.3 m deep had developed on its rear face before it was heightened and widened by the addition of a mixture of chalk and surface scrapings incorporating occupation material. The latter included pottery of earlier Iron Age types.

The interior is covered with trees, shrubs and undergrowth, often dense in places. It was deliberately planted when the fort and its environs were incorporated in the enlarged park of Amesbury House. Certainly by 1773 (Andrews and Dury) the interior was laid out in a pattern of

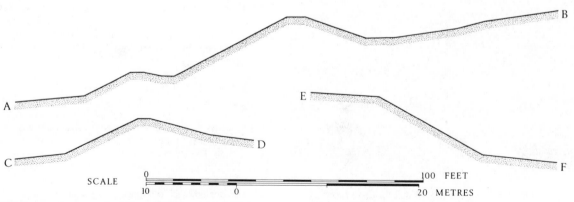

Fig. 13a. VESPASIAN'S CAMP, profiles across defences

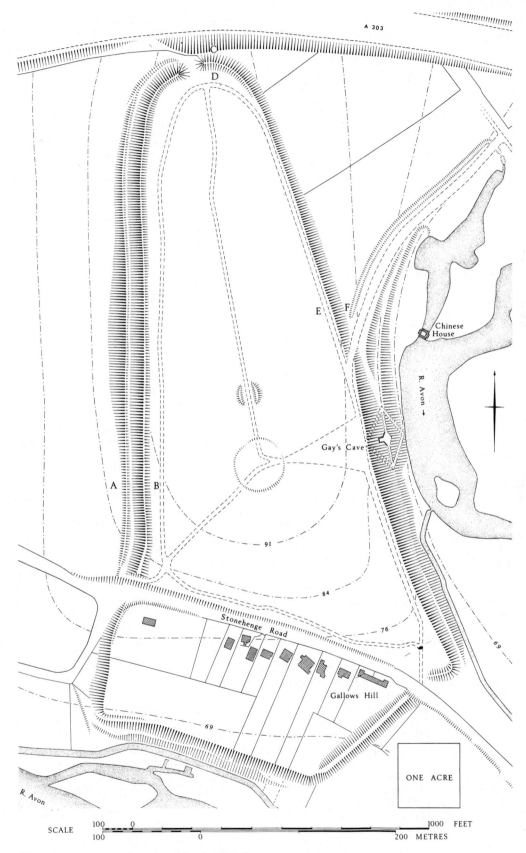

Fig. 13b. VESPASIAN'S CAMP, Iron Age hill-fort

trees and rides which has persisted little altered to the present. Before emparking it was under the plough as may be seen in Stukeley's drawings of 1723 (Stukeley 1740, Tab. xxvi). A map and accompanying schedule, dated 1726 (wro 944/1 and 2, map 6) shows that the portion n of Stonehenge Road was one of the unenclosed arable fields of Amesbury known as Walls Field, a name which occurs as early as 1613 (wro 283/92). Earlier documents, from 1397 onwards, mention acres 'upon' or 'within' the Great Walls and the Little Walls; terms which appear to distinguish the parts of the hill-fort which lie n and s of Stonehenge Road respectively and which also imply the presence of the road across the fort at that early date (Pugh 1947, *passim*). Cultivation of Walls Field appears to have ceased by 1742 (wro 283/6).

Two barrows within the hill-fort were dug in 1770, probably in the course of landscaping the interior (*WAM* xxviii (1913), 115; xlii (1926), 350-1). The remains of one of these (Amesbury 25) appear to survive on either side of the central n-s ride which has cut through and removed much of the mound (14604173). It has been suggested that the second barrow (Amesbury 24) stood at 14614167 but there is now no visible mound at this point which lies within a roughly circular level platform some 50 m across. The series of walks or rides within the hill-fort converge at this latter feature (*see* Andrews and Dury) and suggest that it is the product of mid eighteenth-century landscaping.

Enclosure (109421), almost totally flattened by ploughing, lies ssw of Fargo Plantation among the remains of 'Celtic' fields on a gentle se slope. It appears on air photographs (nmr su 1042/10/272-3; cuap ang 27-8) as an irregular ditched oval about 90 m long (sw-ne) and 45 m across with faint traces of indeterminate internal features. A boundary ditch, which approaches the enclosure from the n, follows the curve of its ditch for a short distance on the e side and then continues sw; it would appear to be structurally later than the enclosure but integrated with it and also with the 'Celtic' fields (p.26).

Probable enclosure on Stonehenge Down (119416), completely levelled by ploughing, appears as a soil-mark on air photographs (nmr su 1339/1/024-5; 1141/14/91; 1141/19/433; os 70 067: 142-3; cuap rc 8 cm 123). It is d-shaped with rounded corners and encloses about 1 ha (3 acres). There is no clear evidence of a bank, nor of an entrance. An examination of the site while under the plough revealed no surface finds.

AMESBURY/WINTERBOURNE STOKE

Bronze Age settlement at Longbarrow Cross Roads was found during construction of the roundabout in 1967. Excavation revealed: four circular structures, probably later Bronze Age huts, sw of the long barrow in the ne quarter of the former cross roads (09974145); several small shallow pits containing pottery of comparable date, a short distance away just s of the A303; and two stockade trenches, possibly part of the settlement, one running n-s in a wide curve just w of the old alignment of the A360, the other approximately e-w around 09964135 (interim report in *WAM* lxiii (1968), 108). Air photographs (nmr su 0941/2/26-9; 1041/8) show a small rounded enclosure, some 65 m by 85 m, cut by the A303 a little further w (09784140), possibly part of the settlement; they also show traces of what appears to be a large but incomplete rectangular enclosure (centre 09864166), mostly in the nw quarter of the cross roads. The latter is undated but appears to respect the adjacent round barrows. 'Celtic' fields e of the settlement are possibly to be associated with it.

BERWICK ST JAMES

Enclosure (09653915), on the se slope of a ridge immediately n of Druid's Lodge has been levelled by ploughing but is visible as a ditched feature on air photographs. It has the appearance of two conjoined curvilinear enclosures without a common division measuring 190 m by 110 m overall and enclosing about 1.6 ha (4 acres). There is no obvious entrance. One air photograph (nmr su 0939/12) suggests the presence of numerous pits over the whole of the interior. There are traces of 'Celtic' fields around the enclosure, especially to the n and ne, and of a smaller enclosure or ring immediately to the ne.

nmr su 0939/1, 10-12. cuap rc 8 bv 11-12.

DURRINGTON

Excavations in 1951-2, in 1966-8 and in 1970 have revealed extensive traces of Late Neolithic occupation to the n, w, and s of Durrington Walls. Sherds of Grooved Ware, intrusive in the ditches of later monuments, are recorded from a linear ditch (15204409), some 150 m to the n (Wainwright and Longworth 1971, 310, 318), from the ditch of a round barrow (Durrington 65b) 18 m to the s (Stone, Piggott and Booth 1954, 164), and from a ditch terminal (15134344) some 16 m further s (Wainwright and Longworth 1971, 47). Sites defined by structural features are described below.

Three pits and a ditch (14764364), 20 m w of Durrington Walls, and a fourth pit (14734355), 98 m further to the sw (Wainwright *et al.* 1971, 78-82, 94-9). The pits, circular or irregular in plan, measured 1.48 m to 0.90 m in diameter and 0.60 m to 0.14 m in depth. The ditch, running n-s, traced for a distance of 15 m and extending beyond the excavated area, was 0.26 m wide and 0.20 m deep; it may have defined the limit of features represented by five undated post-holes on its e side. Finds included sherds of Grooved Ware, two scrapers and other worked flints, bone points, antler picks, bones of domestic pig, ox, sheep and dog, a roe-deer antler with skull fragment attached, and a limpet shell. Radiocarbon dates of 1527 bc ± 72 (bm-703) and 1647 bc ± 76 (bm-702) were obtained from bone and antler in one of the pits.

Post-holes and occupation debris (15134349), alongside the s bank of Durrington Walls (Stone, Piggott and Booth 1954, 166-8). The post-holes, around 0.30 m in diameter and not exceeding 0.45 m in depth, formed for the most part a double row, traced for a distance of 20.7 m; there were three short offsets to the s. The posts, not erected to retain the bank, were still standing when it was constructed. An occupation layer containing sherds of Grooved Ware, worked flints, much animal bone, and charcoal had formed on top of the bank talus along the line of posts.

Holes, possibly representing another timber structure (15204343), 64 m s of Durrington Walls (Wainwright and Longworth 1971, 44-7). The plough-eroded holes, often irregular in shape and rarely exceeding 0.3 m in depth, are tentatively interpreted as 18 post-holes and a pit; they were traced over an area 18.2 m by 10.6 m. Eleven holes, along the N and W sides, formed a roughly rectilinear plan. Finds comprise sherds of Grooved Ware, worked flints and fragments of bone.

Late Neolithic occupation extending about 150 m SSE from Woodhenge was uncovered during Mrs M. E. Cunnington's excavation of the four ring-ditches aligned along the edge of the high ground above the River Avon (Cunnington 1929, 41-8, pl. 39). The ring-ditches, Mrs Cunnington's Circles 1-4, are presumed to represent ploughed-out round barrows, Durrington (67-70), although only the late-stage Beaker grave at the centre of (67) provides unambiguous evidence of function or date. Fragments of Grooved Ware found low in the ditches of (67), (69) and (70) seem best interpreted as debris derived from a pre-barrow settlement associated with the pits and post-holes described below. Re-examination of the finds in Devizes Museum has clarified the date of these features, as follows.

Eight 'holes' (Barrow (67), Circle 1; 15134323), probably post-holes, measured 0.45 m to 0.25 m in diameter and 0.33 m to 0.17 m in depth; five formed a NNW-SSE alignment. Finds comprised: sherds of Grooved Ware, a bone point, worked flints (an arrowhead, a scraper and a flake), a flint hammerstone, bones of ox and pig, and charcoal.

Post-holes (Barrow (68), Circle 2; 15134326), 27 in number, 0.15 m to 0.30 m in diameter and 0.10 m to 0.28 m deep, generally spaced at intervals of 0.75 m, appear to have defined part of a fenced enclosure truncated by the barrow

ditch. The surviving part, irregular in plan, measured approximately 6 m by 10 m by 9 m, with a gap 3 m wide in the NE side. Features within the fenced area comprised a single post-hole, four pits, and a shallow grave containing the crouched skeleton of a female with dolichocephalic skull. Two more pits, one containing a deposit of cremated bones, lay on the line of the fence and a further two outside it. The pits, ranging in diameter from 1.0 m to 1.8 m, and in depth from 0.58 m to 1.57 m, yielded: sherds of Grooved Ware, a flint arrowhead, bones of ox, pig, sheep and dog, and charcoal. It is uncertain whether the unaccompanied inhumation, and the cremation, deposited centrally in the upper fill of a pit and apparently associated with sherds of Grooved Ware and ox bones, are to be related to the barrow or, as their positions may suggest, to the Neolithic settlement.

A shallow pit (Barrow (69), Circle 3; 15114328) near the inner edge of the ditch contained a sherd of Grooved Ware, a flint scraper, bones of ox and pig, and a piece of fired clay.

Middle Bronze Age settlement (150432) immediately S of Woodhenge lies at 100 m OD on the summit of a spur which falls steeply to the River Avon on the east. Situated within the former open-fields of Durrington it had long been totally flattened by ploughing when discovered from the air in 1926. Photographs revealed a small egg-shaped, ditched enclosure about 23 m in diameter with an entrance 6 m wide on the SSE. From the W side of the entrance the enclosing ditch

Plate 16. Ditches S and W of WOODHENGE, Bronze Age enclosure ('Egg') in foreground: view from SE during drought of 1976.

continues SSE for 24 m to join a linear earthwork. Excavations (Cunnington 1929) showed that the ditch varied in section but on average was 2.1 m wide at the top, 0.3 m at the bottom and 1.1 m deep. South of the entrance, post-holes at intervals along the ditch suggested the former presence of palisading. Over half the interior was excavated revealing a number of pits and post-holes, some possibly the remains of a building. One of the pits contained charred grains of barley. Part of a Barrel urn and a rusticated body sherd came from the ditch, but the paucity of finds suggests that the enclosure may have been for stock rather than for human habitation.

Mrs Cunnington suspected that the enclosure was only part of a larger settlement site but it was not until the drought of 1976 that it proved possible to confirm her supposition. Air photographs taken then show as parch-marks a number of additional features (Pl. 16). Attached to the NNW side of the enclosure is a smaller, roughly circular enclosure with gaps in its encircling ditch, while to the s of it, almost touching the linear earthwork, is a small square enclosure. Larger rectangular ditched enclosures, some overlapping and, therefore, of different phases, lie w, N, and E of the main enclosure and one at least is attached to it. A broad trackway defined by parallel ditches leads towards the enclosure from the NNW.

Other traces of Middle Bronze Age activity around the enclosure are more explicitly indicative of domestic occupation. A pit (15044325) exposed by a pipe-trench c.1950 contained the lower part of a Barrel urn (Stone, Piggott and Booth, 1954, 165-6). The same trench brought to light fragments of Barrel and Globular urns, together with animal bones, when it passed through the ditch of a small round barrow (Durrington 74; see Barrow Excavations). Comparable pottery came from the upper levels of the ditch of another barrow (Durrington 68), where it was incorporated in a mass of dark soil containing animal bones, part of a sarsen quern, a hone and a fragment of clay daub with wattle impressions. (The pottery, originally attributed to the Iron Age (Cunnington 1929, 46), was erroneously thought to be associated with the late Neolithic fenced enclosure cut by the barrow.) A few sherds (unpublished, in Devizes Museum) were also recovered from the top of the outer ditch of a third barrow (Durrington 67).
NMR SU 1443/10-13; 1543/167-9.

Iron Age occupation remains (15154380) were found within the henge at Durrington Walls during road construction in 1966-7 (Wainwright and Longworth 1971, 312-28). Excavation revealed five pits, one of them probably a storage-pit 2.1 m deep, the remainder shallower; also four post-holes and a linear ditch. The latter, of which only the very base survived, crossed the excavation from SW to NE and its full extent is unknown. Further s a narrow palisade ditch, probably also of Iron Age date, cut the neolithic Southern Circle from E to W. Another seven pits were exposed by a pipe-trench in 1950-1 in the same area (Stone, Piggott and Booth 1954, 158, 164, 174-5).

Packway Enclosure (152441) of late Iron Age date, sited at the summit (107 m OD) of an E-facing spur overlooking a bend of the River Avon, was discovered and partially excavated during road construction in 1968 (Wainwright and Longworth 1971, 307-28). Kite-shaped in plan, with

four straight sides of unequal length varying between 42 m and 70 m, it was defined by a ditch v-shaped in profile, some 3.6 m wide at the lip and 2.1 m deep from the surface of the chalk. The entrance was a narrow gap in the shortest (s) side. Ploughing had completely removed the presumed internal bank of the enclosure and had severely eroded the interior in which only two pits, each less than 1 m deep, were found.

A linear ditch of later Bronze Age date aligned NNE-SSW met the SE corner of the enclosure; it measured up to 1.5 m across and 0.9 m in depth and was v-shaped in profile. A large undated 'working hollow' was found immediately E of the ditch.

Romano-British settlement and traces of earlier occupation have been discovered immediately SW of Durrington Walls around 147435. Pits, trenches and much Romano-British pottery had been noted in 1918 (Farrer 1918, 101). In 1970 excavations carried out in advance of tree-planting within an area some 300 m by 25 m revealed an extensive spread of pits, post-holes and gullies (Wainwright *et al.* 1971). No house structures were detectable but building tile and some dressed stone in rubbish pits suggests the former presence of a building nearby. It was concluded that the main nucleus of the settlement lay on higher ground to the west. Remains of two small ditched enclosures, one containing a corn drying kiln, were found around 14704354, and to the SW two infant burials. A broad shallow ditch appears to have marked the limit of the settlement on the N around 14744361. Pottery from the site, a mixture of New Forest, Oxfordshire and more locally produced wares, is mostly of the late third and fourth centuries but a small amount is assignable to the second century. Two shallow pits yielded early Iron Age pottery.

Romano-British pottery including samian, probably the remains of a settlement, was found sometime before 1930 on either side of Fargo Road on Durrington Down at 12374372 (Cunnington 1930, 186).

WILSFORD CUM LAKE

Enclosure on NW slope of Rox Hill (120387), now almost levelled by ploughing. It is perhaps to be identified with the settlement in this area recorded by Hoare (1810, 213) who, on digging, 'found the usual *indicia* of ancient population'. No finds survive from his excavation nor have any been found during field-walking, a dearth which suggests the possibility that the site might be of the Bronze Age, rather than the Iron Age as has been suggested (VCH *Wilts* I (i), 123). The enclosure is five-sided (Pl. 17), about 35 m across, with a bank and external ditch but no clearly marked entrance. It lies near the SE end of a boundary earthwork which makes a pronounced angle, apparently to encompass it (Map 1). The enclosure and the dyke are integrated with 'Celtic' fields and the former possibly overlies them.
RAF CPE/UK/1811: 2355-6.

Enclosure (13554050) N of Normanton, on an E-facing slope just above a river-cliff on the w bank of the Avon, has been levelled by ploughing but appears as a ditched feature on air photographs (NMR SU 1340/1-2). It comprises four straight sides of uneven length enclosing an area of about 0.6 ha (1½ acres). No entrance is visible.

WINTERBOURNE STOKE

Enclosure (10904255), flattened by ploughing, lies on the

summit of the ridge sw of Fargo Plantation on the parish boundary with Amesbury. It is roughly rectangular in plan, 80 m by 40 m, and is defined on air photographs by a prominent bank; an external ditch is less well marked except along the NW side (Pl. 21). There is no clear indication of an entrance. It is integrated with 'Celtic' fields on the NW side but it appears to overlie others unconformably and it certainly overlies a boundary ditch (p.26) which passes along its w side.

OS 70067: 149-50; CUAP RC 8 CM 144-6; CUAP ANG 27-31.

Square enclosure (101422) of about 1 ha (2¼ acres) on Winterbourne Stoke Down, probably a sheep penning of medieval or later date, has been completely levelled by cultivation. It was probably first ploughed during the second World War. Earlier air photographs (NMR SU 1041/10; 1041/19/6335) show it as an earthwork with a narrow bank and external ditch. There is no obvious entrance.

WOODFORD

Enclosure (104388), on the summit of a spur SE of Druid's Lodge, has been levelled by cultivation but appears on air photographs as a ditched feature. It is roughly circular in plan, about 140 m in diameter, and encloses about 1.6 ha (4 acres). Possible entrances occur on the SW and NNE (NMR SU 1038/3/96-7). Traces of ridge-and-furrow are visible NE of the site.

NMR SU 1038/1/39-40, 1038/2/43-4, 1049/8/171.

Plate 17. Enclosure, 'Celtic' fields and boundary earthwork NW of ROX HILL, Wilsford cum Lake. 1930

BOUNDARY EARTHWORKS AND DITCHES

AMESBURY

Boundary earthwork (12754268-11774213) extends NE-SW for 1.1 km immediately N of Stonehenge. It has been largely flattened by ploughing and much of it is now visible only on air photographs but the NE third survives as a slight earthwork (Pl. 7). The ditch converges on the Avenue from the sw, turns near it and runs parallel before curving away to be lost in ploughed and disturbed ground in Stonehenge Bottom. A section cut at its closest point to the Avenue showed it to be a very small feature at this point, no more than 0.5 m deep. An excavation (interim report in *WAM* lxiii (1968), 108) prior to the construction of the pedestrian underpass at Stonehenge (12184230) revealed a terminal of the ditch that indicated a deliberate break in its line. Here it was of v-profile, 1.2 m wide and 1.3 m deep and had held a stockade of posts about 0.3 m in diameter. Three turf-lines sealed the ditch, the uppermost containing Romano-British pottery and a lower one sherds of 'Late Bronze Age type'. An intrusive crouched burial had been placed in the terminal of the ditch after the posts had decayed.

Beyond the break the ditch continues on the s side of the A344, runs close to the barrow Amesbury (10a) and ends at the edge of a group of 'Celtic' fields, with which it appears to share a common alignment and was perhaps integrated. At 11834214 a second ditch, 350 m long and also flattened by ploughing, meets it from the NNE.

NMR SU 1242/18; 1242/98/109.

Boundary earthwork (13654226-12934124), levelled by ploughing and now visible only as a ditch on air photographs, extends from the top of the Seven Barrows ridge to just s of Luxenborough Plantation, a distance of 1.4 km. It begins as twin parallel banks aligned SE and becomes single at an abrupt change of direction WSW. At this point it is possible that a branch of the ditch extended a short distance further east. Near Luxenborough Plantation the ditch appears to curve to avoid round barrows Amesbury (18) and (118) suggesting that it is later in date, though perhaps still of the Bronze Age. This is probably the ditch referred to by Aubrey (Long 1876, 143): 'Near the Penning aforesaid where the Kings-graves are, is Normanton-ditch, but why so called, no tradition.' The Penning of West Amesbury lay in the valley (127412 approx.) immediately SW of Luxenborough Plantation (Hoare 1810, 198); the 'Kings-graves' are the barrows in and around the Plantation. A probable explanation of the name of the ditch, which puzzled Aubrey because it lay in West Amesbury, is that it is heading southwards towards the boundary of Normanton Farm, formerly a detached part of Durnford parish but since 1885 in

Wilsford cum Lake. Though still visible in the late seventeenth century the earthwork could not be located by Hoare (1810, 198). Most of its course lies within the former open-fields of West Amesbury which, at least by the early eighteenth century and perhaps earlier, were being extended w to encompass this ridge, and which are primarily responsible for its denuded condition.

CUAP RC 8 CM 121-2; NMR SU 1341/7/22-6; 1342/40/89-93.

Ditch (14154193-14284181) w of Vespasian's Camp, now totally flattened by ploughing and visible only on air photographs, extends NW-SE in a straight line for about 180 m. No bank is detectable. The ditch passes close to a number of ploughed-out barrows including a long barrow (Amesbury 140). It lies within the former open-fields of West Amesbury.

NMR SU 1441/18/174-5.

AMESBURY/WINTERBOURNE STOKE

Boundary earthwork (10854272-10824188) sw of Fargo Plantation, runs N-S for some 850 m, in part among 'Celtic' fields with which it is integrated. The rectangular enclosure at 10904255 (p.25) overlies it and N of this the ditch appears to divide into two almost parallel branches. Towards the s it meets the small enclosure centred at 109421 (p.22), follows the curve of its ditch for a short distance then appears briefly to divide and to continue SW.

CUAP ANG 27-31; NMR SU 1042/10/272-3.

BERWICK ST JAMES, WILSFORD CUM LAKE, WINTERBOURNE STOKE

Complex of boundary earthworks extends for over 4 km from w of Longbarrow Cross Roads (096415) to Rox Hill (120386) with extensions NE beyond Normanton Gorse

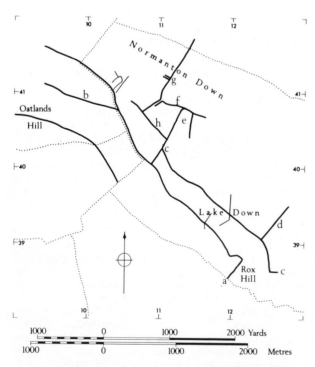

Fig. 14. DIAGRAM of boundary earthworks in Berwick St James, Wilsford cum Lake and Winterbourne Stoke

(114417). The ditches almost certainly represent a number of phases of construction but it is now almost impossible to elucidate these from surface inspection alone. Very considerable portions have been levelled or severely damaged by ploughing and elsewhere tracks and other disturbance have almost always masked the junctions between the various parts. These are described below, though in no sense is a chronological sequence implied. It is suggested, however, that the whole complex was laid out during the Bronze Age, and parts of it probably in an early phase of that period.

The main through boundary (a-a) is a substantial earthwork where well preserved; s of Lake Wood, for example, it measures 13.5 m across overall and the bank (on the NE side) stands 1.5 m above the ditch-bottom. Further s near Rox Hill its dimensions are only slightly less. Near Longbarrow Cross Roads the earthwork crosses, and is probably later than, a stockade trench which runs N-s immediately w of the modern road (A360). This trench is possibly a component of the Middle Bronze Age settlement nearby (p.22). The boundary earthwork almost certainly overlies 'Celtic' fields at 103408, but w and NW of The Diamond plantation, around 102410, such fields appear to conform to it. In the latter area a subsidiary boundary (b), now visible as a ditch only on air photographs, joins the main earthwork from the ENE (09404112); it was built on top of the 'Celtic' fields. On Rox Hill the main boundary changes from a gently sinuous course to a series of short straight sections marked by angular changes of direction, apparently to accommodate 'Celtic' fields which lie on either side of it. The pattern here suggests that the boundary was inserted into existing fields rather than laid out with the fields. A small enclosure (p.24), probably part of a settlement, lies within the angle made by the boundary on Rox Hill.

A second main boundary (c-c) runs roughly parallel with the above for a distance of some 2.4 km (11004025-12653863); it survives as an earthwork on Lake Down but NW of this, where it crosses the former West Field of Lake, it has been ploughed flat. North of Rox Hill 'Celtic' fields abut it on the s but do not appear to continue on the N side. Towards the SE end the boundary climbs the steep slope of Rox Hill; at the top it turns sharply E, perhaps to conform to the 'Celtic' fields of which only the merest traces are now visible on air photographs. A further boundary earthwork (d) some 600 m long, meets the main boundary (c-c) from the NE at 12423906; it is probably of later date but the junction of the two is obscured by a later track. It is a slighter work, 7.5 m across overall, and comprises a ditch with a bank along the SE side.

At the NW end (11004025), the main boundary (c-c) turns sharply NE and becomes the w side of a three-sided earthwork (e) generally known as the 'North Kite' (Crawford and Keiller 1928, 254). (Slight remains of a ditch continue this new alignment SW from the turn to meet the boundary earthwork (a-a) at 10874006.) The relationship of the earthwork to barrows of the Lake Group suggests that it is earlier. The disc barrow (Wilsford 45b), though badly damaged, appears to overlie the boundary, which lacks a bank at this point (Fig. 15); and the w end of the double barrow (46) appears to have cut the boundary. Hoare (1810, 211) found that the w mound had been opened before; the E mound yielded objects of Early Bronze Age date.

Most of the 'North Kite' has been levelled, much of it since 1946 (see RAF CPE/UK/1769: 3332) but part of the w

Plate 18. Boundary Earthworks, round barrows and 'Celtic' fields on LAKE DOWN, from the northwest. 1972

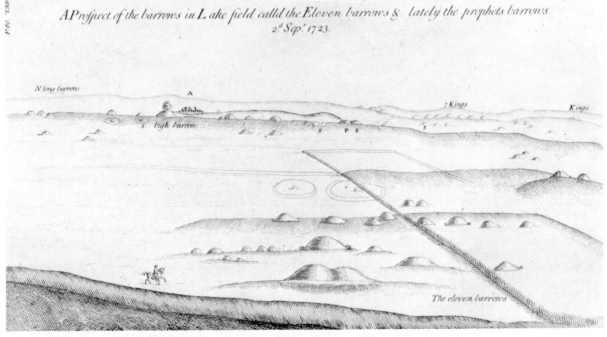

Plate 19. Boundary Earthworks and the LAKE Barrow Group *after* Stukeley (1740, Tab. xxxi), looking NE towards Stonehenge from *c.* SU 107401

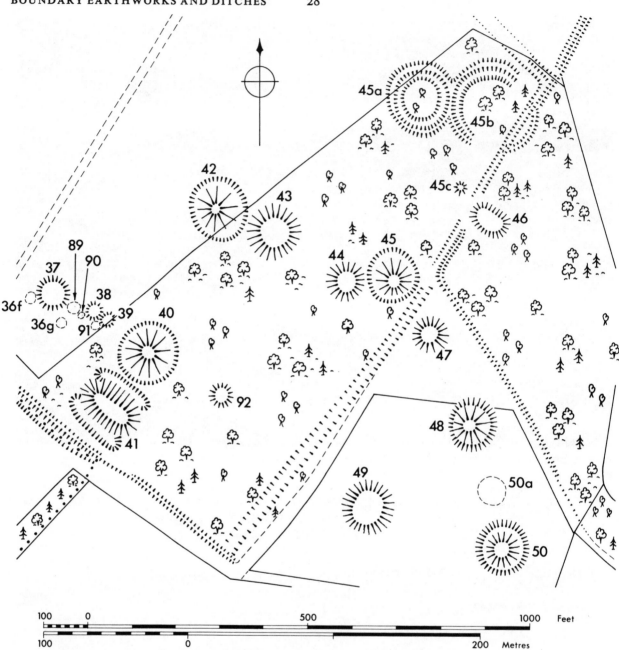

Fig. 15. Boundary earthworks and the Lake Barrow Group

side survives. Just N of the wood in which most of the Lake Group lies is a flat topped bank 4.5 m across and 0.5 m high with traces of a ditch along the w side, but it gradually increases in size until about 100 m N of the wood it is 8.5 m wide and up to 1.7 m high from the west.

In 1958 a small number of exploratory cuttings were made in the earthwork (interim report in *WAM* lvii (1959), 229). One (no location given) revealed pottery of Early Bronze Age date in the buried soil, sealed by the bank; two cuttings on the s produced no evidence that the earthwork was closed by a bank and ditch on this side. A cutting on the E side, showed a narrow ditch (also visible on some air photographs) just E

of the main ditch and parallel to it. It is linked on the N to a similar ditch which extends for some 600 m ESE-WNW (1158407 1-1100408 7), and which utilises in its course the ditch of the N side of the 'North Kite'. At the w end this ditch turns sharply sw and runs parallel for over 100 m with a further boundary (g) forming what appears to be an entrance to a large enclosure.

The boundary earthwork (g) runs NE-SW for 1.2 km (1146417 1-1074407 5) from beyond Normanton Gorse to the E edge of The Diamond plantation where it meets a further boundary (h) which extends NW from the w side of the 'North Kite'. Most of (g) has been levelled by plough-

Plate 20. Boundary Earthwork on WILSFORD DOWN (w side of 'North Kite'), looking NE from SU 11124045 towards Bush Barrow. 1978

ing; at 11154120 short lengths of twin parallel ditches about 20 m apart meet the earthwork from the w but there is no gap in its course to support the idea that they are part of an entrance.
RAF CPE/UK/1811: 2355-7; RAF 106G/UK/915: 3204-5; OS 70 067: 77-81, 142-6; CUAP RC 8 BV 9-12, 24-5; NMR SU 0941/7/86-9; 1041/26/84-5; 1041/27/91-2; 1041/31/59-62.

BERWICK ST JAMES/WINTERBOURNE STOKE
Boundary earthwork (08904070-10403978), now levelled by ploughing and visible as a ditch on air photographs, extends NW-SE for 1.8 km. Towards its w end on Oatlands Hill (beyond the area mapped here) it skirts two small enclosures and appears to cut a ring-ditch. East of the Salisbury-Devizes road (A360) it lies unconformably across 'Celtic' fields and is almost certainly of later date.
CUAP RC 8 BV 11-13; RAF 3250: 10-11; NMR SU 0940/1/ 239-44; 2940/3/185-7.

DURRINGTON
Ditch (10604430-10694431) now levelled by ploughing, runs w-E immediately s of two round barrows (Durrington 1 and 2) adjoining the boundary with Winterbourne Stoke.
NMR SU 1044/4-6.

WILSFORD CUM LAKE
Ditches (10404115), now visible only on air photographs, and of very narrow dimensions, form a partial 'enclosure' around the long barrow Wilsford (34). The group of ploughed-out round barrows (Wilsford 35-36e) lies just outside the enclosure to the southeast. The ditches appear to share a common alignment with 'Celtic' fields just to the N and were, perhaps, integrated with them. One of the ditches appears to be cut by a major boundary earthwork at 10314105. A further ditch (10374100-10544119), also levelled, extends NE from The Diamond plantation and appears to be later than round barrows of the group mentioned above.
CUAP RC 8 BV 10-12; NMR SU 1041/26/84-5; 1041/27/91-2.
   Ditch (12003963-11853925) on Lake Down, now totally levelled by ploughing, extends s and then SE from near the barrows of the Wilsford Group to those of the Lake Group, a total distance of 460 m. The ditch appears to cross a major boundary earthwork at 11983939.
NMR SU 1139/5/199-201; 1139/6/264-5.
   Ditch (11753941-11663920) on Lake Down, now almost flattened by ploughing, extends SE then s for about 240 m on the w side of the Lake Group of barrows. It appears to be crossed by a major boundary earthwork at 11653926.
NMR SU 1139/8/141.

'CELTIC' FIELDS

AMESBURY, DURRINGTON, WINTERBOURNE STOKE
'Celtic' fields (centre 110435), almost entirely flattened by ploughing, are visible on air photographs around the N fringes of Fargo Plantation. On the w side of the plantation the fields appear to have been laid out over the E end of the Lesser Cursus and probably contributed to its flattening. A number of elongated, probably complete, fields are visible E of the plantation; elsewhere the remains are less clearly preserved. Approximate area 32 ha (80 acres).
CUAP RC 8 CM 144-6, 168-9; RAF 106G/UK/915: 4205-6; NMR SU 1049/8/167-8; 1043/1/4, 5; 1044-1; CUAP SE 54.

AMESBURY, WINTERBOURNE STOKE

'*Celtic*' *fields*, now largely flattened by ploughing, extend E-W for nearly 1.5 km s of Fargo Plantation (104422-117422). The group is a complex one showing no single orientation; the elongated nature of some of the fields suggests that they have been created by the removal of former internal divisions. On the N the fields end at a definite boundary formed by a lynchet running E-W; on the E they appear to go no further than a boundary earthwork (p.25). A boundary earthwork runs N-S through the fields and is aligned with them (p.26). A rectangular enclosure at 10904255 (p.24) overlies the boundary earthwork and also the fields. Approximate area 60 ha (150 acres).

CUAP RC 8 CM 123-5; CUAP ANG 27-31; OS 70 067: 146-8; NMR SU 1041/11; 1049/8/168-9; 1142/15.

BERWICK ST JAMES, WILSFORD CUM LAKE, WINTERBOURNE STOKE, WOODFORD

'*Celtic*' *fields* survive intermittently over a large area between Druid's Lodge and Longbarrow Cross Roads (103390-102415) but throughout have been flattened or severely reduced by ploughing. Air photographs suggest that they were once continuous. At the N end fields lie on either side of the long boundary earthwork which extends from the cross roads SE towards Rox Hill. Those SW of the earthwork around 102410 appear to be laid off it or to conform to it, although a spur joining the main boundary appears to cut the fields at 103408; those NE of the earthwork, around 102414, are on a quite different alignment. Further S, around 104403, fields appear to have been cut by the main boundary earthwork and by another one running parallel to it on the west.

Throughout much of this area, and especially in Winterbourne Stoke, air photographs reveal a palimpsest of cultivation; modern ploughing overlying ridge-and-furrow in furlongs, in turn overlying 'Celtic' fields. Total area at least 128 ha (320 acres).

OS 70 067: 77-9; CUAP RC 8 CM 124-6, BV 10-12; RAF 58/3250: 0009; NMR SU 0939/5/209; 0941/7/86-8; 1040/2/22; 1041/10; 1041/19/6337; 1041/27/91; 1041/28/100.

DURRINGTON

'*Celtic*' *fields* occur in two areas on Durrington Down:
(i) Around 115447 there are a number of low E-W lynchets running parallel but few complete fields. To the SW around 114444 air photographs indicate an irregular, and not original, pattern of fields. Approximate area 28 ha (70 acres).

Plate 21. 'Celtic' Fields and associated features SW of FARGO PLANTATION, looking north. 1966

(ii) Around 121444 is a better preserved group, relatively little ploughed, with some lynchets still 1 m high and several complete square fields. The elongated fields present are not certainly original and have, perhaps, lost internal divisions. Romano-British pottery found immediately SE of this group probably represents a settlement associated with a phase of cultivation of the fields. Approximate area 32 ha (80 acres).

CUAP RC 8 CM 167-8; NMR SU 1043/1/5-6; 1144/1.

WILSFORD CUM LAKE/WOODFORD
'*Celtic*' *fields* survive on the N and W slopes of Rox Hill around 122389. They have been modified by later, probably post-medieval, strip ploughing along the contour. Most of the fields lie between two boundary earthworks; the southern of these is integrated with the fields and makes angular changes in direction apparently to conform to them. Hoare (1810, 213) found evidence of settlement on Rox Hill, un-dated but probably prehistoric, of which the enclosure at 120387 (p.24) probably constitutes part. It appears to overlie one phase of the 'Celtic' fields. Approximate area 24 ha (60 acres). Further remains of 'Celtic' fields occur on the NE slopes of a dry valley around 119382. Approximate area 16 ha (40 acres).

RAF CPE/UK/1811: 2355-6; CUAP RC 8 BV 24-5; NMR SU 1238/3.

WILSFORD CUM LAKE
'*Celtic*' *fields*, now completely flattened by later cultivation (around 130407), are just detectable on air photographs NW of Normanton. They are confined to two modern fields but were presumably once part of a wider pattern.

CUAP RC 8 BV 8-9.

Plate 22. 'Celtic' fields, boundary ditches and ridge-and-furrow revealed by modern ploughing S of WINTER-BOURNE STOKE Cross Roads *c*. SU 100408. 1970

MISCELLANEOUS

AMESBURY
Earthworks of a road, apparently unfinished, survive in pasture N and NE of Stonehenge (11924287-12904230). They comprise a markedly straight alignment NW-SE in two sections defined for the greater part by twin parallel banks and are first recorded as earthworks on OS 6-inch 1st ed. surveyed 1877-8. The NW section was at that time about 290 m long but ploughing since 1959 has effectively flattened 120 m at the NW end beyond bell barrow Amesbury (43), the berm and ditch of which are crossed by the banks. A gap of 320 m, in which there is no trace of the earthworks, separates this section from that to the SE. The latter is some 550 m long. To maintain a gradient suitable to wheeled traffic, especially coaches, it crosses Stonehenge Bottom by means of a cause-way and ascends the slope on either side in a deliberately constructed hollow way. The lack of hollowing elsewhere

within the banks suggests that the road was little used, if at all, and in support of this it may be noted that no gaps were cut through the Cursus to accommodate the road on its alignment projected to the NW. The road has clearly been responsible for damage to the berm and ditch of barrow Amesbury (43) and for some infilling of the latter. Whether this is due to wear or to the construction of the road is not certain but the latter would seem more likely.

The maximum width of the roadway within the banks is 9 m; the banks themselves are 3-4 m wide, up to 0.6 m above the interior and 0.4 m above the exterior. The apparent absence of side-ditches, both on the ground and on air photographs, reinforces the idea that the banks are the product of material from the roadway. The causeway is a substantial feature some 90 m long, 13 m across overall with a maximum road width of 4 m, and up to 1.5 m high.

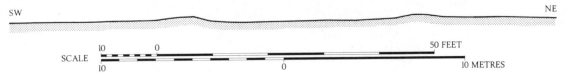

Fig. 16. Eighteenth-century road, profile N of Stonehenge

The alignment of the road projected SE shows that it met, or would have met, the main road w from Amesbury (A303) immediately s of the New King Barrows (13434201), a point which coincides with the SW corner of the former park of Amesbury House. The park was enlarged and extended to this point by the 3rd Duke of Queensberry, probably c.1765 (p.xx), a process which necessitated the re-routing of the public road from Amesbury to Market Lavington. The line of this latter road lay across the corner of the enlarged park and is still visible as a crop or soil-mark on numerous air photographs (e.g. NMR SU 1342/36; 1342/40/92-3). Ogilby (1675, pl. 32) shows it passing among the Seven Barrows (i.e. King Barrows), and Stukeley (1740, Tab. XXIV), more precisely, between the northernmost pair of the New King Barrows.

Roads in the Amesbury area were turnpiked in the earlier 1760s and by 1773 (Andrews and Dury) the Amesbury-Shrewton road passed Stonehenge on its present line (A344). No road, however, is shown on this line in Stukeley's drawings (Tab. III and XXVIII) and Ogilby's map shows that in 1675 the Shrewton road passed some distance N of Stonehenge.

Andrews and Dury show a road or track probably on the line of the earthworks under discussion as, also, does the map of Amesbury Hundred published by Hoare (1826), although no such track is shown on his earlier maps (Hoare 1810, between pp.112-13 and 170-1) or on OS 1-inch 1st ed. surveyed 1810. By 1823, as a sale map of the Amesbury Estate shows (WRO 283/202), the down immediately w of the New King Barrows was in arable, and by implication any route across it was no longer in use; certainly none is shown.

Pewter hoard, probably Roman, was found during plough- ing (130414 approx.) and recorded by Aubrey (Long 1876, 143):

'Near the Penning aforesaid (i.e. West Amesbury Penn- ing), where the Kings-graves are, is Normanton-ditch, but why so called, no tradition. In the field thereby hath been found, by ploughing, within 30 years last past (*sc.* about 1638 or 1640) as much Pewter as was sold for five pounds. The shephard had pitcht through it in many places in pitching for their Fold. It was pure pewter, here were not any Coines found.'

The penning though no longer in existence in Hoare's time was found on enquiry by him (1810, 198) to have been 'in a little vale between tumuli 134 and 137'. These numbers given by Hoare (Pl.I) relate to barrows now numbered Amesbury (17) and (19a) and show the penning lay in the valley between them at about 127412.

Plate 23. STONEHENGE DOWN looking SE along 18th-century road, the Cursus obliquely in foreground. 1977

The 'Kings-graves' are presumably the barrows in and near Luxenborough Plantation and 'Normanton-ditch' would appear to be the boundary ditch, now levelled, which extends NNE-SSW along the E side of the Plantation (p.25).

Two post-holes about 30 m apart were revealed in 1968 by an electricity cable-trench which ran between 'King Barrow Wood' and Stonehenge; exact positions are not given in the interim reports (*WAM* lxiv (1969), 123; lxviii (1973), 61; *Archaeological Review* ii (1968), 6). The holes had supported posts about 0.56 m in diameter; a sherd of Late Neolithic pottery (type unspecified) was incorporated in the chalk packing round one of the posts.

Three circular pits (possibly post-holes: 12054237, 12064237, 12084237), lying some 253 m NW of the centre of Stonehenge and aligned approximately E-W, were revealed by excavation in 1966 in advance of an extension of the car-park (Vatcher and Vatcher 1973); their positions are marked in the surface of the tarmac. At the time they were tentatively assigned to the Neolithic period. More recently, radiocarbon dating by samples of pine, a species suggestive of an early post-Glacial period, from two of the holes, gave dates of 7180 bc ± 180 and 6140 bc ± 140, indicating points in the Mesolithic period (information kindly given by Major H. L. Vatcher).

Unidentified earthworks were recorded by Hoare (1810, 170):

'There are also near them [i.e. barrows Amesbury (39b) and (39c)] under the hill, some appearances of earthen works much mutilated, which I cannot account for: I once thought they formed part of a circle, but I cannot speak with any decision about them.'

It is not clear exactly where these lay, whether between the barrows and Vespasian's Camp about 146422, or to the SE about 148419 where Hoare shows (Pl. 1) what appear to be earthworks. Scrutiny of available air photographs has failed to produce any clear indication of the earthworks mentioned.

ABBREVIATIONS

CUAP Cambridge University Air Photograph
DOE   Department of the Environment
NMR   National Monuments Record, Royal Commission on Historical Monuments (England)
OD   Ordnance Datum (height above mean sea level)
OS   Ordnance Survey
PPS   *Proceedings of the Prehistoric Society*
RCHM Royal Commission on Historical Monuments (England)
VCH   Victoria History of the Counties of England
WAM *Wiltshire Archaeological and Natural History Magazine*
WRO   Wiltshire County Record Office, Trowbridge

BIBLIOGRAPHICAL REFERENCES

Andrews and Dury. Andrews, J. and Dury, A. *Map of Wiltshire*, 1773. Reprinted: Wiltshire Archaeological and Natural History Society, Records Branch, viii, 1952. Devizes.

Annable, F. K. and Simpson, D. D. A. (1964) *Guide Catalogue of the Neolithic and Bronze Age Collections in Devizes Museum*. Devizes.

Ashbee, P. (1963) The Wilsford Shaft. *Antiquity* xxxvii (1963), 116-20.

Ashbee, P. (1978) Amesbury Barrow 51: Excavation 1960. *WAM* lxx-lxxi (1975-6), 1-60.

Atkinson, R. J. C. (1979) *Stonehenge*. Harmondsworth.

Atkinson, R. J. C. and Evans, J. G. (1978) Recent excavations at Stonehenge. *Antiquity* lii (1978), 235-6.

Bonney, D. J. (1976) Early Boundaries and Estates in Southern England. *In* Sawyer, P. H. (ed.), *Medieval Settlement*. London.

Burleigh, R., Longworth, I. H. and Wainwright, G. J. (1972) Relative and absolute dating of four late Neolithic enclosures: an exercise in the interpretation of radiocarbon determination. *PPS* xxxviii (1972), 389-407.

CBA *Radiocarbon Index. Archaeological Site Index to Radiocarbon dates for Great Britain and Ireland.* Council for British Archaeology. 1971-7. London.

Christie, P. M. (1963) The Stonehenge Cursus. *WAM* lviii (1961-3), 370-82.

Christie, P. M. (1970) A round barrow on Greenland Farm, Winterbourne Stoke. *WAM* lxv (1970), 64-73.

Clark, R. M. (1975) A calibration curve for radiocarbon dates. *Antiquity* xlix (1975), 251-66.

Clarke, D. L. (1970) *Beaker Pottery of Great Britain and Ireland*. Cambridge.

Crawford, O. G. S. (1929) Durrington Walls. *Antiquity* iii (1929), 49-59.

Crawford, O. G. S. and Keiller, A. (1928) *Wessex from the Air*. Oxford.

Cunnington, M. E. (1914) List of the Long Barrows of Wiltshire. *WAM* xxxviii (1913-14), 379-414.

Cunnington, M. E. (1929) *Woodhenge*. Devizes.

Cunnington, M. E. (1930) Romano-British Wiltshire. *WAM* xlv (1930-2), 166-216.

Cunnington, M. E. (1935) Note on a burial at Amesbury. *WAM* xlvii (1935-7), 267.

Cunnington, W. and Goddard, E. H. (1896) *Catalogue of Antiquities in the Museum of the Wiltshire Archaeological and Natural History Society at Devizes. Part I: The Stourhead Collection*. Devizes.

Defoe, D. (1928) *A Tour through England and Wales*. (First pub. 1724-6) Everyman edition. London.

Farrer, P. (1918) Durrington Walls or Long Walls. *WAM* xl (1917-19), 95-103.

Goddard, E. H. (1913) A list of prehistoric, Roman and pagan Saxon antiquities in the county of Wilts. arranged under parishes. *WAM* xxxviii (1913-14), 153-378.

Grimes, W. F. (1964) Excavations in the Lake Group of Barrows, Wilsford, Wiltshire, in 1959. *Bulletin of the Institute of Archaeology* (University of London) iv (1964), 89-121.

Hoare, R. C. (1810) *The History of Ancient Wiltshire. Part I*. London.

Hoare, R. C. (1826) *The History of Modern Wiltshire. Part II (ii): Hundreds of Everley, Ambresbury, and Underditch*. London.

King, A. N. (1970) Crop-mark near West Amesbury. *WAM* lxv (1970), 190-1.

Laidler, B. and Young, W. E. V. (1938) A surface flint industry from a site near Stonehenge. *WAM* xlviii (1937-8), 151-60.

Long, W. (1876) Stonehenge and its Barrows. *WAM* xvi (1876), 1-244.

Lukis, W. C. (1864) Danish Cromlechs and Burial Customs. *WAM* viii (1864), 145-69.

Merewether, J. (1851) Diary of the Examination of Barrows and other Earthworks in the Neighbourhood of Silbury Hill and Avebury. *In* Archaeological Institute of Great Britain and Ireland (Salisbury meeting, 1849). *Memoirs illustrative of the History and Antiquities of Wiltshire and the City of Salisbury*. London.

Moore, C. N. (1966) A possible Beaker burial from Larkhill, Durrington. *WAM* lxi (1966), 92.

Ogilby, J. (1675) *Britannia*, i. London.

OS Map of Neolithic Wessex. 2nd ed., 1933. Southampton.

Pugh, R. B. (1947) *Calendar of Antrobus Deeds before 1625*. Wiltshire Archaeological and Natural History Society, Records Branch, iii. Devizes.

RCHM (1970) Royal Commission on Historical Monuments (England). *An Inventory of Historical Monuments in the County of Dorset, ii: South-East*. London.

Roe, F. E. S. (1966) The Battle-Axe Series in Britain. *PPS* xxxii (1966), 199-245.

Ruddle, C. S. (1901) Notes on Durrington. *WAM* xxxi (1900-1), 331-42.

Shortt, H. de S. (1946) Bronze Age Beakers from Larkhill and Bulford. *WAM* li (1945-7), 381-3.

Smith, G. (1973) Excavation of the Stonehenge Avenue at West Amesbury, Wiltshire. *WAM* lxviii (1973), 42-56.

Stevens, F. (1919) Skeleton found at Fargo. *WAM* xl (1917-19), 359.

Stone, J. F. S. (1938) An Early Bronze Age grave in Fargo Plantation near Stonehenge. *WAM* xlviii (1937-9), 357-70.

Stone, J. F. S. (1947) The Stonehenge Cursus and its Affinities. *Archaeological Journal* civ (1947), 7-19.

Stone, J. F. S. (1949) Some Grooved Ware pottery from the Woodhenge area. *PPS* xv (1949), 122-7.

Stone, J. F. S., Piggott, S. and Booth, A. St J. (1954) Durrington Walls, Wiltshire: recent excavations at a ceremonial site of the early second millennium BC.

Antiquaries Journal xxxiv (1954), 155-77.

Stone, J. F. S. and Young, W. E. V. (1948) Two pits of Grooved Ware date near Woodhenge. *WAM* lii (1947-8), 287-306.

Stukeley, W. (1740) *Stonehenge: A Temple Restor'd to the British Druids*. London.

Stukeley, *Diary*. Family Memoirs of the Rev William Stukeley. . . iii (Lukis, W. C., ed.). *Publications of the Surtees Society* lxxx (1885).

Thurnam, J. (1870) On Ancient British Barrows, especially those of Wiltshire and the adjoining Counties (Part ii: Round Barrows). *Archaeologia* xliii (1870), 285-552.

Vatcher, F. de M. (1961) The Excavation of the Long Mortuary Enclosure on Normanton Down, Wilts. *PPS* xxvii (1961), 160-73.

Vatcher, F. de M. (1969) Two Incised Chalk Plaques near Stonehenge Bottom. *Antiquity* xliii (1969), 310-11.

Vatcher, L. and Vatcher, F. de M. (1973) Excavation of three post-holes in Stonehenge car park. *WAM* lxviii (1973), 57-63.

VCH *Wilts*. The Victoria History of the Counties of England. *A History of Wiltshire* I (i), 1957; I (ii), 1973; IV, 1959. London.

Wainwright, G. J., Donaldson, P., Longworth, I. H. and Swan, V. (1971) The excavation of prehistoric and Romano-British Settlements near Durrington Walls, Wiltshire, 1970. *WAM* lxvi (1971), 76-128.

Wainwright, G. J. and Longworth, I. H. (1971) *Durrington Walls: Excavations 1966-1968*. Reports of the Research Committee of the Society of Antiquaries of London No. xxix. London.

INDEX

Where necessary for ease of identification, page references to principal entries are given in bold type.
Barrow numbers are quoted in parentheses.

Stonehenge from sw, condition in 1904. Fenced road in foreground crosses monument. Fallen trilithon (re-erected 1958) immediately beyond.